## 100 PLANT-INSPIRED RECIPES
### TO RECONNECT YOU WITH YOUR BODY AND THE NATURAL WORLD

TARA LANICH-LABRIE—creator of *The Medicine Circle*—credits plants and the natural world with saving her life. After experiencing years of chronic health issues and pain, she eschewed the prescriptions that weren't working for her, finding her way to health by growing, foraging, and creating healing food with plants. From nettles—her favorite plant—to butterfly pea flowers, mushrooms, lilacs, roses, and more, Tara draws on ingredients both foraged and cultivated to create gluten-free, low-sugar dishes with medicinal benefits. Tara shares her vibrant recipes along with the potential physical and mental health benefits, historical use, and so much more on social media, her website, and in her courses.

Now in her debut cookbook, *Foraged & Grown*, Tara assembles some of her most vibrant, flavorful dishes for you to cherish and enjoy. Almost defying reality with their naturally derived color and beauty, Tara's recipes are lush with joy and nutrients. With her guidance, you can craft Nettle & Butterfly Pea Flower Donuts, Porcini Mushroom & Oat Pasta, Roasted Dandelion Root "Coffee," Cucumber & Purslane Salad, Rose Roll-Out Cookies, and more. Featuring her Essential Plant Glossary and resources on how to build your herbalist pantry, this book invites you to cook with whimsy and affection for the natural world around you.

**FORAGED & GROWN**

# FORAGED & GROWN

## Healing, Magical Recipes *for* Every Season

### TARA LANICH-LaBRIE

**Countryman Press**

*An Imprint of W. W. Norton & Company*
*Independent Publishers Since 1923*

Copyright © 2024 by Tara Lanich-LaBrie

All rights reserved
Printed in Thailand

For information about permission to reproduce selections from this book, write to Permissions, Countryman Press, 500 Fifth Avenue, New York, NY 10110

For information about special discounts for bulk purchases, please contact W. W. Norton Special Sales at specialsales@wwnorton.com or 800-233-4830

Manufacturing through Imago
Book design by Laura Shaw Design
Production manager: Devon Zahn

Countryman Press
www.countrymanpress.com

An imprint of W. W. Norton & Company, Inc.
500 Fifth Avenue, New York, NY 10110
www.wwnorton.com

978-1-68268-832-8

1 0 9 8 7 6 5 4 3 2 1

*This book is dedicated to my daughter, Nila Marina,*
*my Moon, my greatest muse and inspiration,*
*expert taste tester, and teacher.*
*I love you infinitely.*

# CONTENTS

## Fall

## Winter

## Homemade Pantry Through the Seasons

# INTRODUCTION

"You must do something to make the world more beautiful."
—BARBARA COONEY

"YOU CAN EAT ALL OF THIS?!" I exclaimed, savoring my first bite of a puffball mushroom, simply sautéed in butter with a sprinkle of salt, and cooked to a golden crisp over a little camp stove in the back bed of my ecology teacher's pickup truck. This was the moment the world opened up to me.

Everything I knew about food up until this point in my 18 years dictated that all mushrooms and plants growing around us were either poisonous or weeds, and that all herbs outside the culinary herbs in my kitchen cabinet were potentially "snake oil" remedies.

Standing in the little trail parking lot of an arboretum outside Chicago, Illinois, my life changed forever. In that first bite, I tasted flavor I had no name for, and the promise of an infinitely more delicious and novel world. This was not the bland button mushroom that occasionally showed up in my meals; this was an umami taste of revelatory connection to the greater natural world.

"Yes, you can eat this," my teacher said with a laugh.

The Illinois summer sun was casting dappled shadow-leaves across the parking lot we stood in, the thrum of insects undulating in waves through the humidity. I scanned the area, noticing every plant around us had a shimmer of verdant potential; even the dandelions coming through the cracks in the asphalt seemed to be glowing.

"What about cattails?" I asked, pointing to the least-likely-to-be-edible candidate.

"Yes!"

"Dandelions?"

"You can eat the whole plant, actually," she answered, laughing again.

I had nibbled dandelion flowers as a kid, but suddenly the enigmatic landscape outside my door was open; the veil had lifted. Not only could you eat wild plants and mushrooms safely, but they contained multitudes: new flavors, colors, a whole realm of healing and culinary magic I had never touched.

Maybe you're wondering how I didn't know any of this, or maybe you know exactly how I was feeling. I grew up outside of Chicago and my family loved the outdoors. We ate fresh, frozen, or canned vegetables that came from the grocery store; I had never eaten such plants as dandelion greens or nettles. I was introduced at a young age to a wide variety of foods because of my parents' love of food and our proximity to the city's diverse food culture, but foraging and herbalism were not part of my vernacular.

I grew up in awe of the natural world, and have vivid memories of sitting under the lilac bushes in my backyard, a canopy of blooms above me, having an innate sense that everything was right in the dirt with the plants. I was particularly drawn to color: the vibrant purples, blues, and oranges in the flowers around our house, or the subtle variations of green in the deciduous trees that lined our street. I had a photo album filled with the leaves I'd gathered in my neighborhood, with their common and Latin names written below, and collections of rocks and shells, bones and seaglass.

And as I got older, plants and the natural world became more than an interest—I believe they saved my life. I had a number of chronic and autoimmune health issues, and was in a near-fatal car accident a few weeks after I turned 18. For several years, every day, I had debilitating migraines and body pain, often unable to stand up once I sat down. Although I pushed through the days, I felt far older than my years. I was prescribed medications with serious side effects, some of which, I was told, I would need to take for the rest of my life. After trying many of these medications with little improvement, I knew I had to look elsewhere to navigate what I was experiencing.

I began researching, trying different healing diets and methods, eliminating and reintroducing different foods. I felt markedly better when I was not eating gluten, dairy, or sugar—as you might notice in this book, gluten-, dairy-, and sugar-free dishes are still a key part of my diet. But at the time, I missed the food I loved, so I began to experiment with different flours, lower-glycemic sweeteners, and dairy-free options. I also combed through cookbooks, books on herbalism and traditional medicine practices, and began to teach myself to forage, seeking remedies in the natural world.

Around this time, I enrolled in a program to become a naturalist, focusing on ecology, biology, plant identification, and conservation. The classes were mostly outdoor courses on 1,700 acres of Illinois forest and prairie, with ponds and rivers dotting the landscape. There were more than 222,000 plants representing 4,650 different plant species; it was a wonderland, a sanctuary where I felt more myself than anywhere else. I spent every free moment wandering there, and this is when the plants became my teachers, my counsel, my friends.

I began taking medicinal herbs, such as feverfew and willow bark, and my migraines disappeared almost entirely within three weeks. I was awestruck at the healing I was experiencing, and it inspired me to add more plants and flowers in my daily cooking, and to learn to grow food and medicinal plants. I became particularly enamored with nettles, a plant that has a long history of medicinal use all over the world.

It was clear to me that food was now much more than sustenance for me; it served as creative expression, healing, and an offering to the friends at my table, to the land, to myself, and to my ancestors. I love the alchemy of plants becoming food, becoming magic, becoming the spell whispered over my shoulder: "Pick those roses and add them to the batter; infuse this cream with spruce tips; dig that dandelion root to roast for the winter!"

Color is one of the most essential components in the food I create—stirring in deep hues of purples, greens, and blues to help convey the story of the plants and flowers. I find that there is healing in color, like part of the essence of the plant itself, inviting us to experience the plant in our food as if we were coming upon it growing in nature. Color has always been a muse for me; I attended college for painting and art history in Santa Fe, New Mexico, creating colorful, large-scale, abstract landscape paintings composed entirely of thousands of perfect, layered circles in various sizes. To this day, I see circles as a fundamental form in nature, a lens to the moon and sun, expansion and contraction, microscopic cells, plants, the earth itself. My paintings, much like my cooking now, were a way to transmute suffering into something beautiful, a vibrant landscape embodying the macro- and microcosmic world all at once. This is where the name for my business, The Medicine Circle, originated.

I had always dreamed of growing my own food, and after college, I apprenticed with a farmer, learning to grow, harvest, and work with the plants. In the years that followed, I went to graduate school in Colorado and met my now-husband, Mark. We moved to rural New Mexico to start a small farm, selling weekly shares of vegetables and fruits, along with my kitchen creations, such as Nettle "Champagne" (page 84), herb- and flower-infused desserts, and homemade pantry items.

I gave birth to my daughter, Nila, and began teaching, foraging, cooking, and baking professionally, bringing everything back to my home kitchen to experiment. I started sharing photos on social media, under the handle @themedicinecircle, of recipes I was creating, stories of what was happening on our little farm, and found an incredible online community of food lovers and plant people. The Medicine Circle began to form as a dream of creating a bridge to the natural world through food.

Foraging in Ireland

I felt that if people could fall in love with dandelions, nettles, and other wild foods, maybe they would turn their attention to the world outside, to their community, and start protecting and/or healing themselves and the land around them. I dreamed of a community online that connected people through a love of food and the natural world, one where everyone was welcome and we could learn together. The Medicine Circle became a way to create connection in a time of increasing isolation and separation from the natural world and one another.

This book is about the plants outside our door, the world we are part of; the tapestry of color conveyed in every spring leaf, the heady fragrance of summer blooms, the rustling stalks of fall seeds, the crystalline signs of winter on every spruce needle. This book is about building a bridge to that world.

This is a book for everyone. Whether you are an expert forager, gardener, or herbalist, or you are just starting your journey; whether you have gluten or dairy allergies and want to try something new, or you are just curious about food or plants in general—this book is for you. May you find awe in the world outside your door and inspiration from the recipes in these pages.

## BECOMING A PLANT PERSON

When you become a forager, herbalist, gardener, or plant enthusiast, you find yourself falling in love with the natural world over and over; you celebrate first blooms and new leaves like the arrival of an old friend. And equally, you mourn the inevitable loss and cycles that nature embodies.

Your vision starts to shift, encompassing not just the one or two plants you see as you're walking down the street, but the community of flora you step in to every time you leave the house. You begin to mark seasons by what is going to seed or fruit, and you may start to "feel" the plants before they appear. You bring gifts and offerings in your pockets when you visit to harvest the first dandelions, and it is not officially spring until you smell the first violet or eat your first bowl of nettle soup. You are attuned to the seasons and the plants begin to seek you out. It may be a subtle nudge at first, or like some kind of synchronistic magic.

This is not something reserved for plant whisperers or master herbalists; anyone can learn—this is part of who we are. Human beings have been interacting reciprocally with plants since the beginning of our time. Plants are ancient, community-oriented beings; we are 499 million years younger, and can learn so much from our elders.

All our ancestors, whether recent or distant, were foragers and herbalists, and we carry that imprint somewhere inside us. Our body contains thousands of receptors for specific plant compounds, and over the course of our lives we build a catalog of reference points based on flavor, texture, sight, and feel of all the plants we encounter and eat.

To build a deeper connection to the plants, we must expand our vocabulary of relational knowledge, approaching them with curiosity as we would a new friend. Embodied experience far surpasses scanning a post on social media or reading a plant identification book.

Research and learning are essential tools, especially with plants, but the quality of direct experience can deliver us to the dandelion in our backyard in wholly different ways. Connecting in this way to the plants around us, wherever we live, can bring immeasurable healing to not only ourselves, but to the entire community of plants, humans, and other living beings.

The simplest way to begin is by sitting with a plant for 3 minutes, observing, sharing a breath: our inhale of oxygen is their exhale and their inhale of carbon dioxide is our exhale; this small act opens the door to deeper connection, healing, and inspiration.

If this sounds far-fetched, that's understandable. You do not need to have an earth-shattering experience to harvest a dandelion, but I urge you to pay attention to the changing landscape in one small space. It could be a 4-by-4-foot balcony space in your apartment building. It could be your backyard dandelions, grass, and rosebush. It could be a lilac on your morning walk to work. It could be your local park, or someplace out in the wilderness. How does it change day by day? Observe the space for a few days, weeks, or months; take a photo, jot down some words, record a voice memo, or simply watch. What birds or pollinators do you notice? Make an offering, begin to create a reciprocity with the plants. What happens when a flower blooms and then goes to seed? What are the ways the landscape changes from March to July to November?

Maybe you will observe something that shifts your perspective, or maybe it will be a moment to take a breath with the natural world; both are just right.

## HOW TO USE THIS BOOK

This book is arranged to take you on a journey through the plants and into the seasons, beginning with the fresh, verdant spring plants and winding into the warming, comfort foods of winter. I created these recipes to invoke the essence of each month from spring, summer, fall, and winter, weaving a tapestry of magical food from what is growing and what has been preserved.

You will find "Simple Swaps" and "Forager's Notes" attached to many of the recipes. The swaps are there to make each recipe accessible for nearly any season or place, no matter where you live in the world. The notes highlight ways to harvest or work with the plants, flowers, or mushrooms included in the recipes.

We will explore how to begin building a culinary herbalist's kitchen and pantry, and move into colorful, plant-focused meals, drinks, and desserts. All recipes in the book are made without gluten and can be made without dairy, and most are sweetened with maple syrup, honey, or coconut sugar. I have been cooking in this way for many years for health reasons and share more about this in the pages that follow.

We will eat from the land around us, wherever we are in the world, beginning to attune to the subtle shifts that are occurring all the time in nature. Foraged and seasonal foods

Summer Lilac Honey                    Nettle leaves

grow in a community, and they contain the story of the terroir, the weather, plants, mycelium, and soil.

We are all coming from different places in the world, so our options will vary depending on the time and place. Many ingredients in this book can be dried or preserved to use later, purchased from a local farmer, or even found online, and I have shared some favorite sources where you may buy the more esoteric or harder-to-find ingredients, if you are interested.

Foraging is a path of deep connection to the plant world, and it is essential be respectful when harvesting. There are endangered and threatened plants that should never be harvested when foraging, and you should never harvest from small patches of plants or plants that you do not know. Only gather small amounts of any plant from a community of plants, and always use what you harvest and share what you make. Sit with a plant and ask permission; consent is the foundation of working with the plants and it is important to not harvest when you don't feel a strong "yes" from the plants. Bring a gift or offering in exchange, in gratitude for what is being shared with you.

Although *Foraged & Grown* is not a plant-identification book, and the information it provides is not intended to diagnose, treat, or prevent any condition, my hope is that you will find inspiration in these pages to step in to your landscape in new ways, to engage with the magic in the world where you live and bring it back to your kitchen, finding healthful, delicious ways to connect with the natural world.

# BUILDING THE CULINARY HERBALIST'S PANTRY

## PANTRY ESSENTIALS

This is a list of ingredients I keep stocked in my pantry most of the year, and many of these ingredients are used throughout the book. There is an array of dried plants, mushrooms, and flowers to add color and beauty, flavor, medicinal benefits, nutrients, and minerals. I also powder my herbs, flowers, and mushrooms to add to such recipes as doughnuts or sauces, and this allows for quick and easy additions to regular meals. Everything in the book is gluten- and dairy-free and most things are preserved or sweetened with either maple syrup, coconut sugar, or honey. To be able to cook these recipes, I would recommend stocking up on the following ingredients more regularly:

COCONUT FLOUR: Coconut flour is very dense, so a little goes a long way. It can be excellent for baking and is a favorite for people who are grain-free. It is high in healthy fats and protein.

OAT FLOUR: Oat flour is a favorite of mine because it is easily made at home, accessible, and inexpensive. Oats are also a medicinal herb, and the flour is quite versatile. Some people are allergic or sensitive to oats, especially if they have celiac disease, and sorghum flour is often a good replacement.

GARBANZO BEAN FLOUR: Garbanzo bean flour is used all over the world to make savory gluten-free foods. It is made from ground garbanzo beans (also known as chickpeas or besan) and is a favorite for its buttery, slightly nutty flavor and smooth texture, lending itself to savory pancakes and battered, fried foods.

NUT FLOURS: In this book, I use almond, chestnut, and hazelnut flours. All three flours are ground from the nut in their name; in many of the recipes, they can often be used interchangeably. However, almond flour tastes mild and buttery, whereas chestnut and hazelnut flours are much stronger in flavor. They all work well combined with other gluten-free flours and in baked goods.

**BUCKWHEAT FLOUR:** Buckwheat is gluten-free, and it is technically the seed of a fruit, making it what is called a pseudocereal. It is a good source of fiber, is rich in minerals, and has an almost nutty flavor. Buckwheat helps increase glutathionine, a powerful antioxidant; it may be anti-inflammatory and anticancer, and has been used to help lower cholesterol and balance blood sugar.

**CORNMEAL AND MASA:** Cornmeal is dried corn, ground to different consistencies. In this book, the cornmeal is ground fine for the recipes shared. Masa is also corn, but it has been nixtamalized, an ancient process from Aztec culture, of boiling corn with ashes or slaked lime, also called cal, that strips the corn of the pericarp, the outer casing of the kernel, and alchemizes the corn into an extremely delicious, nutrient-dense food. Masa flour is very different in texture from cornmeal and cannot be substituted.

**TAPIOCA FLOUR AND STARCH:** Tapioca is derived from cassava root, but is made up of only the starchy part of the plant. It is an excellent thickening agent and helps provide a glutinous feel to baked goods.

**SWEET WHITE OR "GLUTINOUS" RICE FLOUR, A.K.A. MOCHIKO:** Sweet rice flour is not literally glutinous, but is made from sticky rice, giving it a higher starch content than other rice flours. It is excellent for building body and structure in gluten-free baking and is also the essential ingredient in mochi.

**SORGHUM FLOUR:** Sorghum is a grass seed that is ground to make a mild and lightly sweet flour. It is an ancient grain from Africa that has been used for more than 5,000 years. It can replace oat flour and works well in baked goods.

**FLAXSEEDS:** Flaxseeds are high in fiber, omega-3 fatty acids, and lignans. They can be ground and mixed with water to make an egg substitute for some baked goods.

**MAPLE BUTTER:** Maple butter contains no butter at all; it is maple syrup cooked down and reduced to a soft and creamy spread. I use it frequently as a glaze and icing for baked goods. It dries glossy and tastes like maple syrup. Creamed honey will often work to replace maple butter, but it will have a sweeter taste and slightly different texture.

**MAPLE SYRUP:** Pure maple syrup is my favorite sweetener, and it is my primary source of sugar in baking. Maple syrup has been used for hundreds of thousands of years and was first made by Native Americans by boiling the running sap of the sugar maple tree. It is fairly high in manganese and riboflavin, and small amounts of calcium, potassium, and zinc. The syrup also contains antioxidants, so although it is definitely sweet, it adds a depth of flavor and has beneficial properties.

HONEY: This is another favorite sweetener that has been used for thousands of years as a preventative and curative medicinal. Honey has been used as a powerful antiviral and antibacterial, and is employed in many hospitals outside the United States for burns and wound healing. I use honey to preserve and add flavor to a number of dishes throughout the book, for medicinal remedies, as well as in desserts and dressings.

COCONUT SUGAR: Coconut sugar is harvested from the sap of coconut palm flowers, and it is slightly lower on the glycemic index than cane sugar. It has a light caramelized flavor, similar to that of brown sugar, and can be replaced with cane sugar in any of the recipes in the book.

NETTLES: I drink regular infusions of nettle all year-round, and I powder it in a spice or coffee grinder to use in baked goods, pasta, smoothies, and other recipes. I keep nettle leaf dried in sealed jars for use through all the seasons. It adds color, medicinal properties, and bright flavor to everything it touches. Nettle powder is one of my most used pantry items. I also reserve at least an 8-ounce jar of nettle seeds to use as a garnish and energizing addition to meals. Nettles are an adapto-genic plant, meaning they are known to support the body in lowering stress levels and increasing energy. Learn more about nettles on page 30.

ROSE PETALS: Fragrant, unsprayed rose petals are essential in the culinary herbalist's pantry. They have so many uses, from garnishing to powdering and flavoring, as well as adding to both sweet and savory dishes. Roses are a flower of the heart, and they are an astringent, cooling, and gentle herb that has been used for thousands of years across the world.

ROSE HIPS: I love to have this sweet "fruit" of the rose, dried and seeded for use in both powder and whole forms. Rose hips must be seedless if used in a powder form, and strained if they have seeds, as the seeds themselves contain irritating hairs. Rose hips are extremely high in vitamin C and add a vibrant and lightly citrus flavor to both savory and sweet meals. Learn more about rose hips on page 33.

MARIGOLDS: Marigolds are one of my favorite edible flowers, both dried and fresh, because they retain their vibrancy and color when dry and in baking. I love the deep orange marigolds for a pop of sunshine in the winter months, and they have been used as a medicinal herb for hundreds of years in several different cultures.

BUTTERFLY PEA FLOWERS/POWDER: Butterfly pea flowers are my favorite culinary and medicinal flower. They are one of the only naturally blue edible flowers in the world. They contain large amounts of anthocyanin, an antioxidant that is known to support heart health. They are adaptogenic, and have been used as a brain tonic and aphrodisiac in Ayurvedic medicine and other traditional medicine practices for more than 4,000 years.

LIQUID CHLOROPHYLL CONCENTRATE: This is a deep green, natural concentrate that I use to color things brighter shades of green, to bring people into the full story of such plants as nettles. It is often made from nettles or alfalfa, both rich sources of chlorophyll.

## HERB AND FLOWER POWDERS

My most oft-used kitchen tool is an old electric coffee grinder, with a worn and handwritten label of "Flowers & Herbs," that I use to grind nettles, seeded rose hips, roasted dandelion root, wild mushrooms, and so much more. One of the most important ingredients in culinary herbalism, seasonal cooking, and my home pantry are the dried herbs I collect and preserve. I live in an area that only has fresh plants and flowers for about five months of the year, so I dry many of my herbs, mushrooms, and flowers to use in the other seven months. Culinary and medicinal herbs and mushrooms provide color, flavor, nutrients, and medicinal benefits to smoothies, soups, baked goods, pastas . . . the possibilities are endless! Any dried herbs or herbal teas can be used, whether they are foraged, grown, or purchased.

To powder your favorite ingredients, start with completely dry herbs, roots, mushrooms, seeds, or flower petals. Not all herbs or petals are perfect for blending, but many will work beautifully. Place about ¼ cup of plant material at a time in a clean coffee grinder, spice grinder, or high-speed blender. Blend on high speed for about 30 seconds, or until the plant material is a fine powder. Place a mesh sieve over a medium bowl, and pour the powdered plant material into the sieve. Tap it until all the powdered material is finely sifted into the bowl. Discard or use any larger leftover bits, and store the powder in a sealed container with a dated label. Use as needed, and enjoy added to your favorite meals and drinks.

NOTE: Plants must be completely dry and cooled before powdering. For example, if you are roasting dandelion root, let it cool completely before blending.

## KITCHEN ESSENTIALS

These are the kitchen tools I have found helpful for processing and preparing seasonal and foraged foods, herbs, and mushrooms. There are always ways to work around things if you don't have the following items, but this list is a good starting place for any foraging and herbalist kitchen.

**COFFEE OR SPICE GRINDER FOR PLANTS:** This is one of the most essential items in my kitchen. I use an old coffee grinder to powder mushrooms, dried flowers, and herbs to add to meals and baked goods.

**DOUGHNUT MOLDS:** I use a nine-doughnut silicone mold made by the Wappa brand for all my cake doughnuts. It is a standard-size doughnut mold and distributes heat well across the bake.

**BAKING SHEETS:** I use baking sheets for everything from drying plants and salts to winnowing seeds, and of course, baking. Baking sheets have a shallow rim that comes up all the way around the perimeter of the sheet.

**BLENDER, FOOD PROCESSOR, OR BOTH:** High-speed blenders are great for getting the smoothest, creamiest textures, and some blenders can grind grains into flour. Food processors are helpful for processing plants and sauces quickly and easily.

**ICE-CREAM MAKER:** If you love ice cream or sorbet, this is a fantastic tool. I have had my ice-cream maker for 13 years and I use it regularly for making ice creams and sorbets with foraged plants and herbs, such as my Spruce Tip Mochi Ice Cream (page 71).

**CAST-IRON SKILLETS:** Cast-iron skillets are the most important kitchen tool I own because they are incredibly versatile and conduct heat evenly. Cast iron can be used for stovetop cooking, baking at high temperatures, and cooking over a fire.

**MORTAR AND PESTLE:** A mortar and pestle are excellent for grinding up spices, pestos, and herbs, and pounding dry and wet ingredients to add to various dishes.

**DEHYDRATOR:** A dehydrator is an excellent tool for drying and preserving the seasonal harvests, both foraged and grown. I run dehydrators all season long to preserve herbs, mushrooms, fruits, and flowers for the off-season. Dehydrators can be an investment, although I have found them inexpensively in thrift stores. But even so, it is not necessary to start drying all your flowers, herbs, or even mushrooms with a dehydrator. Using an oven on the lowest setting, hanging herbs to dry in bundles, or laying out flowers on a dry towel can work just as well. If air drying, be sure they are in a dry, well-ventilated, unlit area. It is important to label all your herbs as they are drying because they can look very different from when they are fresh. Place in airtight containers and label their containers once they are completely dry; most herbs will keep for 6 months to a year in sealed containers out of direct sunlight.

**SHARP KNIVES/KNIFE SHARPENER:** Sharp knives are important when you're cooking or foraging. If your knife is dull, it is much more likely to slip and cause an injury. You can also get thinner and more accurate slices with a sharp knife. Getting a basic knife sharpener is inexpensive and completely worth it. In my everyday cooking, I use a chef's knife, a nakiri knife (a Japanese knife designed for slicing vegetables), and a paring knife. It does not really matter which kind of knife you are using, as long as it is sharp and feels good to you.

MASON JARS IN VARIOUS SIZES: I use mason jars for preserving pickles and medicinal herbs, fermentations, the storage of herbs and dried goods, and to refrigerate, can, or otherwise preserve the seasonal harvest.

| INGREDIENTS | GRAMS PER 1 US CUP | GRAMS PER 1 US TABLESPOON |
| --- | --- | --- |
| ALMOND FLOUR | 100 | 6 |
| OAT FLOUR | 120 | 7.5 |
| TAPIOCA FLOUR/STARCH | 115 | 7 |
| VEGAN/DAIRY BUTTER | 226 | 14 |
| COCONUT OIL, MELTED | 220 | 14 |
| MAPLE SYRUP | 315 | 20 |
| HONEY | 350 | 22 |
| COCONUT SUGAR | 180 | 11 |
| WHOLE OATS | 100 | 6 |
| NETTLE LEAF, FRESH | 22 | X |
| PORCINI MUSHROOM POWDER | X | 7 |
| ROSE POWDER | X | 5 |
| ROSE HIPS, SEEDED | X | 5 |
| BUTTERFLY PEA POWDER | X | 5 |
| BAKING SODA | X | 18 |
| BAKING POWDER | X | 12 |

# MY ESSENTIAL PLANT GLOSSARY

SOME OF THE PLANTS in this book are cultivated in gardens, many are foraged; you can even purchase most online, or at a natural foods store, in their dried form. This book is intended to provide inspiration for creating food with healing, seasonal, and/or foraged plants, but if you cannot find a plant listed in the recipe, there are almost always substitutions available in the vast plant world. The following plants are all featured in recipes in this book. My hope is that this glossary gives you a glimpse into each plant's story, medicine, and magic, so you can appreciate their significance when cooking with them.

ANISE HYSSOP, *Agastache foeniculum*: Anise hyssop is a member of the mint family, is endemic to North America, and has a delicious scent a bit like catnip, anise, cinnamon, and licorice combined. It has been used by Indigenous North American peoples for hundreds of years as a warming digestive aid, a culinary herb, and an antibacterial remedy. It has been used for supporting digestion, and for relief from flus and respiratory ailments. Anise hyssop is used as incense, in protective medicine bundles, and as a medicine to soothe the emotional and spiritual heart. It is a sweet and delicious culinary herb, and I love to infuse it into ice creams and baked goods, use it to make digestive bitters or cough syrup, and dry it for tea.

BILBERRY/HUCKLEBERRY, *Vaccinium myrtillus*: Bilberries are a low-growing little berry of many common names, including but not limited to whortleberries, huckleberries, wind berries, wiwinu, oolalee, American or European blueberries, blaeberry, and fraughans. From Wales to North America, Sweden to Ireland, this little berry is a cherished, late summer forage. It ripens in August, and an ancient harvest celebration in Ireland called Lughnasadh, associated with the god of light, Lugh, includes a community harvest of bilberries, games, matchmaking, and visits to holy wells.

Bilberries are very nutritious, high in heart-protective anthocyanin and vitamin C. They have been used medicinally and as food in Asia, Europe, and North America for digestive disorders, diabetic complications, and eyesight. Harvesting bilberries is best done in a harvest party or as a meditative practice, as it can be a long process to gather enough berries for pie or tarts. With a flavor that tastes like blueberry concentrated and expanded into a tiny, bursting globe, it is more than worth the purple-stained hands and time it takes to fill a basket.

Butterfly pea flower

**BUTTERFLY PEA FLOWER,** *Clitoria ternatea*: Butterfly pea flower is pure color magic in a lightly flavored indigo flower. There is no other flower that imparts the same brilliant blue hue, and it is the rarest color found in food. Color is one of the most important parts of conveying a story in the food I create, a powerful medicine in its own rite. We take in so much information through color, and it is a constant inspiration in my cooking. I once dreamed of having an entire farm of blue and purple foods, but have compromised happily with growing and learning from this plant for the past seven years.

Butterfly pea is a tropical, vining blue flower that has been used medicinally and culinarily for hundreds of thousands of years in Ayurvedic as well as Traditional Chinese and Thai medicine as aphrodisiacs, adaptogens, and for its neuroprotective, liver, and heart effects. The flower has been used as an antimicrobial, inflammation-reducing mild analgesic, and can be helpful with chronic pain. Imparting a brilliant blue color to everything it touches, changing from deep indigo to bright fuchsia, depending on the pH levels in the surrounding medium, it never ceases to amaze. Over time, it has become one of the most important ingredients in my kitchen. I have grown butterfly pea flowers as annual plants in my garden in the southwestern United States for more than seven years now, and they can grow perennially in tropical locations.

**BURDOCK ROOT,** *Arctium lappa*: Burdock is often viewed as a weed plant, with giant clumps of sticky burrs clinging to everything that brushes up against it. They were the inspiration for the original Velcro; the seed-containing burrs are a brilliant evolution, spreading easily across the world.

Burdock is prized for its edible and medicinal root that has been used for millennia, eaten throughout Japan and other parts of the world as a salad vegetable, fried, and added to stir-fry dishes. In addition to being a staple vegetable, it is used to cleanse the liver and blood, and to aid in digestion, as well as heal the skin and decrease excessive inflammation in the body. Burdock grows prolifically in disturbed soil or fields, mountains, and most other landscapes; it is a survivor and is not easily deterred. In its second season, it will produce flowers and the trademark burrs. Burdock is one of my favorite culinary medicinal roots, and I harvest it each fall; it has a slight artichoke flavor and goes perfectly in soups and stews, sautés, and salads. Burdock can be found in the wild and it can be grown in gardens.

CALENDULA, *Calendula officinalis*: Calendula holds the sun in its ray florets, bringing summer with it into every sip of tea or bite of a petal-filled cookie. It has been used traditionally as a liver and skin tonic and as an antiviral and antimicrobial. It is a very resilient plant and will grow in most

Calendula

places, being drought resistant and cold hardy. Calendula is a perfect garnish fresh or dried, and it is one of the flowers I use most often. It was known as "poor man's saffron" in times past because of its brilliant orange petals and less costly price. The resinous green bottom of the flower holds the most medicinal value, so be sure to leave this intact if possible when adding to teas, infusing oils, or making broths. Every fall, I make several quarts of calendula-infused olive oil to use as a soothing body oil, a little sunshine drizzled over winter salads, or an extra addition to dressings. Calendula grows happily in pots on a windowsill or planted in the earth.

CHOKECHERRY, *Prunus virginiana*: Chokecherries are little stone fruits, drupes, with a fascinating history of use; they are endemic to North America, and the bark, twigs, and fruit of chokecherries have been used extensively by First Peoples for food, medicine, and ceremony for millennia. The Pueblo people of North America have used chokecherries as a treatment for many ailments, from coughs and congestion to digestive issues, pain relief, and as a powerful sedative. The cherries were and are used as a main source of food, providing much-needed calories, vitamins, and anthocyanin. Chokecherries are dried in the sun, added to soups, or pounded into pemmican, a thick nourishing cake that can be stored and eaten easily all year.

Chokecherries do contain cyanogenic glycosides, so it is necessary to heat the bark, fruit, and leaves for at least 15 to 20 minutes to deactivate the cyanide; this

Chokecherries

is also the case for apple seeds, cherries, apricots, plums, elderberries, and so on. It would likely take a significant amount of raw seeds to kill a person, but do not let children eat the raw seeds of chokecherries. People have made food from chokecherries for thousands of years, and I love to make a fresh sorbet or delicious syrup when the fruit ripens in the late summer.

**DANDELION FLOWERS, LEAVES, AND ROOTS,** *Taraxacum officinale*: Dandelion is the spring alchemist in a flush of yellow, pulling the first rays of sun into its blooms, and it is the final farewell of fall, sending energy into its roots as the frost settles in. Dandelion is endemic to Asia and has been used for thousands of years; it is an Arabic, European, Asian,

Indigenous North American, and Mexican traditional medicine plant, with the first written evidence of medicinal use in China in 600 BCE. Every part of the dandelion is edible and is used in culinary and medicinal applications worldwide.

It is nutrient dense, high in vitamins A, C, D, B vitamins, and potassium. Dandelions have been used to detoxify the liver, blood, and lymph, and help with bladder issues, infections, pain, and digestive ailments. Dandelions hold court in fields, the cracks of city sidewalks, on high mountains, along coasts and stream banks, and anywhere plants might grow. They contain expansive energy, proliferating across landscapes with a fervent dedication and overcoming years of pesticide use and manicured lawns. They are fiercely resilient survivalists, a medicine for the times. The roots, flowers, and leaves go into many recipes in this book, and they are a delicious addition to any kitchen pantry. Dandelions can be encouraged and grown easily in gardens if you do not have them flourishing around you already.

**ELDERBERRY AND ELDERFLOWER,** *Sambucus nigra*: Elderflowers are one of the ephemeral blooms that come with the early summer months, their star-shaped blossoms illuminated in the sun. The flowers give way to elderberries, a deep purple or blue, finger-staining berry that is an incredibly potent remedy. Elderberry's genus, *Sambucus*, translates to "gift from the gods."

Elder has a rich folkloric history in Celtic traditions, and it is said that if you fall asleep under its branches, you will be whisked into the fairy realms. Ancient Egyptians were found buried with elder medicines, and ancient Greek physician Hippocrates referred to the elder tree as his "medicine chest." Human settlements that first emerged between 48,000 and 15,000 years ago in Italy and Switzerland show evidence that prehistoric humans cultivated the elder tree. Elderberries have been used as a preventative and curative plant medicine, and are delicious in drinks, syrups, tinctures, elixirs, teas, and desserts.

FUCHSIA, *Fuchsia magellanica*: Fuchsia flowers are bright purple and magenta in color, hanging like jewels from bushes, hedges, or potted plants. Fuchsia has a long history of edible and medicinal use that stretches from Mexico to Iran and

Hawthorn flowers

Ireland. Fuchsia is native to South and Central America. The entire plant is edible, including the flowers, leaves, and berries. The berries are rich in vitamin C, and the brightly hued flowers are loaded with anthocyanin. I grow fuchsia in pots to add as a garnish to desserts and salads and have harvested it along the coast of Ireland, awestruck by the amount flourishing there.

The fuchsia "berries," the seed pods left from the flowers, are far sweeter than the flower and make a delicious jam. Fuchsia has been used as a diuretic, a decongestant, and a soothing plant for urinary tract issues. There are approximately 100 varieties of fuchsia, all known to be edible, and the flowers have a crunchy texture, varying in flavor significantly, with some being quite strong and bitter, and some similar to a bite of cucumber. Fuchsia grows wild in many places and can even be grown in hanging pots as an annual plant.

HAWTHORN, *Crataegus*: Hawthorn is a plant friend I have spent many years learning from, and as with nettles, feel certain I have only scratched the surface. Hawthorn berries are luminescent when ripe, red glowing beacons against fluttering dark green leaves. Hawthorn has been used as a heart-healing medicinal herb for thousands of years in both European medicine and Traditional Chinese Medicine; the berries, leaves, and flowers, studied for their beneficial properties, used traditionally in the treatment of heart disease, strengthening of the heart muscle and veins, and for irregular heartbeats, while supporting inflammation reduction. Medicinally, hawthorn leaves,

Hawthorn berries

flowers, and berries are similar in composition, and I love to work with this magical tree in spring and fall, harvesting flowers and leaves along with the ripe berries when the weather shifts.

HOLLYHOCK FLOWERS AND LEAVES, *Althaea rosea*: Hollyhocks are one of my favorite edible plants to grow in the garden, with showy stalks of colorful flowers and palm-size leaves. They are endlessly fun to work with in baked goods, salads, and wraps. The flowers are very mild, with almost no scent or flavor, and they can be baked, or eaten fresh, dried whole for blooming teas, and used in flower confetti. I have loved hollyhocks since I was a child; we grew them in our little backyard garden next to an old raspberry patch. My mother would pick one of the bloomed flowers and one of the unopened buds and use a straight pin to make little dancers out of them, with the bud on top and a full skirt of blooms below.

Hollyhocks have been used medicinally in Traditional Tibetan, European, and Chinese medicine for hundreds of years. During the Crusades, they were used to heal the "hocks" of horses. This is where the common English name stems from: holly meaning "holy," and hocks referring to the legs of horses.

Hollyhocks, like marshmallow (*Althaea officinalis*), are a member of the Mallow family, which has demulcent and soothing properties. The entire plant can be eaten, including the mild-flavored young leaves and the roots.

LILAC FLOWER, *Syringa vulgaris*: Lilac is an incredibly fragrant and ephemeral flower, a plant for remembering and for soothing the heart. It is one of the only fragrant flowers whose scent cannot be captured in an oil or perfume, except through the slow and demanding process of enfleurage. Lilacs, in a flower essence, may help us to move through grief, loss, and the inevitable and constant change that life brings. Lilacs are in the olive family, Oleaceae, and have a history of medicinal use. Lilacs have an astringent and almost bittersweet flavor, and are a wonderful addition in digestifs and ice creams, and to add a beautiful finish to desserts. Lilacs are often cultivated in gardens, although I occasionally find them growing in the mountains where I live in Colorado. They love the sun and require a good amount of sunlight to produce blooms, but they can be grown in many places in the world and are resistant to cold weather and drought.

LION'S MANE, *Hericium erinaceus*: Lion's mane looks a bit like its namesake, with shaggy spines proliferating from its fruiting body. When cut into slices, it looks like a dendritic cross-section of a human brain, hinting at its potential use for neurological health. It has been used for hundreds of years in Traditional Chinese Medicine for various ailments, and recent scientific studies have shown the many benefits of lion's mane, with increasing evidence that it could support treatment of neurodegenerative diseases, decrease inflammation, and relieve anxiety and depression.

Lion's mane has also been used to support and speed up healing time for serious nerve damage. It is a tonic and a nervine mushroom, soothing the digestive and nervous systems.

Fresh lion's mane can have an almost meaty texture and crablike flavor and is a fantastic addition to broths and savory dishes. It is also one of the easiest mushrooms to grow at home, and many companies now sell lion's mane kits, so they can be grown and harvested right on the kitchen counter.

MARIGOLD, *Targetes erecta* and *Targetes patula*: Marigold, an edible plant with bright jeweled blooms have been used for ritual, food, and medicinal preparations in Mexico, India, and Tibet, among other countries. Marigolds are prized as a hardy and protective garden addition: releasing a compound into the soil through their roots that kills damaging nematodes, drawing in beneficial pollinators and repelling pests.

Marigolds can be eaten raw or cooked, including the young leaves, and are also used as a dye plant, exuding a rich color even when dried. I grow them at the ends of my rows of rainbow corn, drying the petals to use all year long. The petals retain their brilliant hue in cooking and baking, and maintain their vibrancy even when dried. Marigolds taste uniquely floral with a slightly bitter endnote, a perfect garnish and nutritious addition to meals. They can be grown easily in both pots and the garden, and if flowers are regularly harvested before going to seed, the plants will continue to produce vibrant blooms for many months.

MEADOWSWEET, *Filipendula ulmaria*: Fields of meadowsweet waft a heady fragrance of floral almond across the landscape, their flowering tops covered in pollen-drunk bees. That delicious scent imparts beautifully to everything it touches. Meadowsweet is highly tannic and astringent, and is a member of the Rosaceae family with a long history of medicinal use. It is one of the sacred herbs of the Celtic druids and has been used across Europe, North America, and other parts of the world in fermented brews and as a topical and internal medicinal. Much like willow and aspirin, it contains salicylic acid compounds and has been used as analgesics, inflammation regulators, and antimicrobials. Meadowsweet imparts a honeyed, floral, and almond taste to desserts and drinks, and it

Meadowseet

underside of its leaves, like a reflection of the moon's silvery rays. Mugwort has been used for women's health, both for regulation of menses and support in menopause, burned as an incense, and used in moxibustion, a form of Traditional Chinese healing in which small cones of mugwort are lit and placed on the body. Mugwort is a nervine, a divinatory and powerful dreaming herb and can induce vivid, lucid dreams. You can use dried or fresh plants for the recipes in this book. Mugwort can be found in nature and can also be cultivated in the garden. This helpful plant is considered an invasive in many places, and it can spread quickly in a garden.

is one of my favorite herbs to add to recipes, holding true even when heated.

MUGWORT, *Artemisia vulgaris*: Mugwort has a long history of medicinal, culinary, and divinatory use. It is known in some places as "the mother of herbs" or croneswort, for its correlation to wise women and crone, an archetypal figure that appears in the folklore of many cultures. Revered for thousands of years, from Asia to North America, Africa to Ireland, mugwort is most likely endemic to Europe and Asia, and now grows prolifically on every continent except for Antarctica. The Latin name, *Artemisia*, is named for the ancient Greek moon goddess, Artemis, considered to be a protector of women. One of the key identifying properties of mugwort is the silvery

NETTLE LEAF, *Urtica dioica*: My love of nettles knows no bounds. I could spend the next 25 years focused on just nettles, and I would only scratch the surface. I was 11 years old when I first ran into a nettle patch on the banks of Lake Michigan, just outside Chicago, my skin bursting into flames as my bare legs hit the leaves. I had never heard of nettles, and yet I felt more curious than afraid when it happened. I remember it left a shimmer, a kind of bookmark in my mind for that moment. This shimmer is something I have come to recognize as an introduction or invitation to a plant or mushroom that will become a close ally and friend. It's a sense of serendipity that I have learned to wholly trust.

Nettles are an ancestral plant for nearly all of us; they have been growing in almost every place on earth for hundreds and thousands of years. They are endemic to Ireland and other parts of Europe, Asia, North

America, and Africa. All parts of the plant have been used medicinally for hundreds of years as a tonic, an adaptogenic remedy for the adrenals, the prostate, urinary tract infections, rheumatic and other kinds of pain, diabetes, and bacterial infections, among other things.

There are over 200 varieties of nettles in the world, and a surefire way to identify them is by their unmistakable sting. Nettle stings are one of the most fascinating aspects of the plant; they are attributed to a variety of compounds found within the trichomes, a glasslike needle structure lining the undersides of the leaves, the petioles, and the stems. Once this trichome is broken, serotonin, acetylcholine, histamine, formic acid, and a cocktail of other chemicals are released into the skin. Interestingly, flagellation with nettle branches—called urtication in reference to its Latin name, *Urtica*—has been done for millennia. This is a practice

Nettles

that may help with pain, and although I would not recommend it, I have done it for many years to alleviate muscle and joint pain.

Nettles are an incredible, underestimated food plant, one of the most nutrient-dense, adaptogenic greens on earth. They are rich in protein, calcium, magnesium, iron, B vitamins, and vitamins A, C, D, and K. Nettles contain cobalt, chlorophyll, trace minerals, potassium, zinc, copper, and sulfur, as well as all the essential amino acids, making them a near-perfect food source.

They have been used to make clothing and fishing nets, and there are many legends, myths, and fairy tales involving the magic that nettles weave. People often liken them to spinach but, in my humble opinion, nettles are a thousand times more delicious and interesting in flavor. They can be cooked, baked, pureed, dried, and blanched to make all manner of sweet and savory meals. Nettles can be found in nature or grown in a garden almost anywhere in the world, with the right amount of water and sunlight; be aware, they will spread easily and can take over a small garden.

NETTLE SEEDS, *Urtica dioica*: As discussed in the previous listing, nettles are one of the most nutrient-dense plants on earth, though often shunned as a weed plant and feared for their fiery sting. All parts of the plant are edible, and if you come across an abundant patch in the fall months, try harvesting a small amount of seeds to add to your pantry. A little goes a long way, and you want to make sure the plants can regenerate themselves and stay vital, so only harvest from an abundant, healthy patch. Nettle seeds are a tonic, supporting the kidneys and adrenal system. They are extremely energizing and have been used throughout history to increase vitality, libido, and overall health. I eat nettle seeds daily and keep a little bowl on the table to sprinkle over food.

**PLANTAIN,** *Plantago*: The first time I tasted minutina plantain, its mineral-rich flavor and near seaweedlike texture transported me to the oceanside. Minutina is endemic to Italy, North Africa, and the Mediterranean. It is also known as herba stella and buckshorn plantain. It has been used in salads and various preparations since at least the 16th century, and although more than 200 varieties of plantain exist in the world, only a few are used regularly in culinary and medicinal preparations. Such varieties as narrow-leafed, ribbed, and buckshorn plantain are high in vitamins A and C, and calcium. Highly tannic, it is used to alleviate inflammation, relieve insect stings, and support skin health. A tea of the leaves is used to treat coughs, sore throats, and stomach and digestive issues. Plantain leaves can be eaten cooked or raw when young, and dried for use in teas, salves, and body oils. Plantain can be foraged or grown in gardens and thrives in a number of climates and soil conditions.

**PORCINI,** *Boletus edulis* or *B. rubriceps*: Every August, our family ventures into the mountains after long, hot days to search for the choice edible porcini mushroom in the cooler mountains. Mushroom hunting together is one of the great joys of sum-

Porcini mushroom

mer, and whether we come home with a full basket or not, it is a perfect day . . . but we do love a full basket! Also known as cèpes, Boletus edulis, B. rubriceps, and other choice boletes are some of the most sought-after mushrooms in the culinary world, and they are a powerful medicinal mushroom in their own rite. They have long been prized for their umami flavor in both dried and fresh preparations and contain a vast array of nutrients, including vitamins C and E, B vitamins, beta carotene, lycopene, and other flavonoids. They are rich in such minerals as iron, calcium, magnesium, copper, phosphorus, potassium, zinc, and selenium. They also have some of the highest levels of the antioxidants glutathione and ergothioneine. Porcini mushrooms can be found growing in a wide variety of habitats throughout China, Europe, and North America, and they are truly one of the most versatile and delicious mushrooms to add to the culinary herbalist's kitchen.

PURSLANE, *Portulaca oleracea*: Purslane is truly a wonder plant, often perceived as a weed that covers the ground in mats of succulent green leaves. It has the highest omega-3 fatty acid content of any vegetable and is full of vitamins A, C, E, and K. It is a mineral-rich ground cover, containing calcium, magnesium, and manganese, of which many of us are deficient. Purslane is a resilient plant, thought most likely to originate in the Mediterranean, and is often found in disturbed soil and abandoned lots, cracks in sidewalks, and thankfully proliferating among many gardens and lawns.

In Traditional Chinese Medicine, purslane has been recognized for hundreds of years for its medicinal properties in treating all manner of intestinal disorders. This is a plant I harvest and eat fresh, grill or sauté, and preserve for use in winter. It is mucilaginous and similar in flavor to cucumber, with a slight citrusy note. Purslane is often found in the wild, and it can be grown and planted in gardens and pots.

REDBUD, *Cercis canadensis*: Redbuds bloom in a rush of inflorescence for just a few weeks every spring. The little blossoms dangle in bursts all across deciduous trees or shrubs. They are a member of the pea family, Fabaceae, and Indigenous peoples of the Americas and Mexico ate and still eat the redbud flowers, seeds, and pods, both raw and cooked. They are endemic to North America, Mexico, southern Europe, and Asia. The crunchy little flowers have a sweet and slightly sour taste and are significantly higher in vitamin C than citrus fruits. I love to add redbuds to capers, baked goods, salads, or soups. Redbud trees and bushes are found in nature, and they can also be grown in backyards.

ROSE HIPS, *Rosa*: Rose hips are the glowing sweet "fruit" of all roses, containing a bundle of seeds enrobed in a fruity, pectin-rich outside. Rose hips may be soft and fiery red when ripe, with a consistency almost like dates around their seeds; some varieties color to a deep purple, almost black. They contain profound amounts of vitamin C, and beneficial amounts of vitamins A and E, B vitamins, and polyphenols. Rose hips were credited for curing a generation of European children of scurvy and other vitamin C deficiency–related illnesses in World War II, as they contain an astonishing 20 times more vitamin C than an orange, one of the highest concentrations of any plant in the world. You can harvest the rose hips from any rose, whether it is wild or cultivated, as all roses are edible.

ROSE PETALS, *Rosa rugosa*: Roses are a medicine of the heart, both the physical and emotional heart, and have a long history of use spanning from ancient Egypt to Persia, China, and Greece. Roses have been worshiped, admired, and held in the highest of praises by poets, artists, chefs, and herbalists for thousands of years. Wild roses are one of my favorite flowers to work with, often producing an intoxicating scent. The wild rose is a five-petaled flower, growing all over the world, often producing the most intoxicating scent; and it is said that

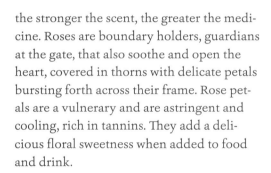

Rose petals

Smooth sumac

the stronger the scent, the greater the medicine. Roses are boundary holders, guardians at the gate, that also soothe and open the heart, covered in thorns with delicate petals bursting forth across their frame. Rose petals are a vulnerary and are astringent and cooling, rich in tannins. They add a delicious floral sweetness when added to food and drink.

SEAWEEDS: All seaweed is edible, making it one of the most accessible and safe plants to forage. Of course, like all plants and mushrooms, some seaweeds are more palatable than others, and there are some varieties that could cause stomach discomfort in some people, but you will not die from eating seaweed. I add seaweeds to broths, salt blends, desserts, salads, and noodle dishes. Seaweeds vary in their nutritional and medicinal properties, but overall they contain significant amounts of iodine,

something most of us don't eat regularly. Seaweed can be an umami flavor enhancer, thickener, and a powerful healing plant. Seaweed must be harvested ethically and at the correct time, as many varieties take a very long time to grow, so please always check local laws, and always have an excellent foraging book on hand.

SMOOTH SUMAC, *Rhus glabra*: Sumac is one of my favorite foraged spices, and it is endemic to North America, the Mediterranean, and the Middle East. Its name is derived from the Arabic word summāq, meaning "dark red," because all the drupes are a deep cadmium red. Sumac has been used culinarily and medicinally for millennia for its antioxidant, antidiabetic, and antibacterial benefits and is high in vitamin C, lightly tart and citrusy, and delicious in everything from desserts to soups to dressings.

SPRUCE TIPS/NEEDLES, *Picea*: Spruce tips are the chartreuse, new growth on a spruce tree in the early spring. They have a citrusy, bright flavor due to significant amounts of vitamin C. They have been used as a powerful medicinal plant, containing shikimic acid, which can help fight the flu and colds, as well as magnesium and high amounts of chlorophyll. Spruce, and all the edible conifers, are a great winter and spring forage.

I love to harvest a small amount of the tender tips in spring, but this beautiful tree is medicine and food all year long. There are several other edible conifers, including fir and pine trees. Know the difference between yew trees and the edible conifers, as yews are deadly poisonous, aside from the red fruit (cone) outside the poisonous seed. Spruce is a favorite for syrups, desserts, salts, creamy foods, and in small amounts, chopped fresh and sprinkled over dishes.

Spruce tips

TULSI, *Ocimum tenuiflorum*: Tulsi basil, also known as holy basil, has been used as a heart-healing and supportive plant in Ayurveda for more than 5,000 years, known as the "queen of herbs," the "elixir of life," and the "incomparable one." Tulsi is endemic to Southeast Asia and India, is an adaptogenic herb, both stress-relieving and energizing, is believed to be anti-inflammatory, antibacterial, and much more. When I travel, I always pack a tulsi alcohol tincture as a support and preventative for flu, colds, and other illnesses. Tulsi is excellent in both culinary and medicinal worlds, adding a unique herby flavor and brightness to anything it touches. Tulsi can be grown in gardens or in pots.

VIOLA, *Viola*: Violas, also known as pansies, were my first taste of an edible flower, after nibbles of dandelions as a child. I came across them as a teenager, and my friend and I ate them sprinkled over watermelon on a playground in a little neighborhood in Chicago. It was a near-ecstatic experience that led me to grow them ever after, wherever I was living in the world.

Violas have a sweet, almost wintergreen flavor, are very mild, and come in a rainbow of variegated hues. They are surprisingly hardy, despite their demure appearance, and I have often harvested blooms both in a Colorado snowstorm and in the baking heat of summer. They grow exceptionally well in small spaces, including pots and balconies, and will continue to bloom for months, as long as they are harvested. They are perfect for drying flat in a book or press, they hold their color in baking, and are delicious as a fresh garnish on cakes, salads, and other savory or dessert dishes.

**VIOLET, *Viola*:** Carpeting the spring forest floor with deep purple and lavender blooms, violets are an aromatic dream. A medicinal and culinary flower, they may evoke a childlike wonder, cause spontaneous outbursts of giggling, or bring forth and help move old grief stored in the body. Historically, violets have been used as a medicinal herb for everything from dry hacking coughs to a poultice for the lymph system, helping alleviate stagnant conditions. There are many different varieties of violets, and there are poisonous and inedible lookalikes, so it is essential to make sure you have the right flower. With heart-shaped leaves, a strong fragrance, and lightly sweet flavor, violets are delicious in desserts, sprinkled on food, or candied in sugar to preserve them. Violets are prolific in some places in the world, and they can be cultivated in backyards quite easily with a particular love of partial sun and well-watered soil.

**WILD PLUM FLOWER, *Prunus*:** In the early spring, I drive with the windows rolled down even when the hand of winter hasn't loosened its grip entirely, inviting the plum blossoms to move through the car in wave after wave of intoxicating scent.

Wild plum blossoms are one of the most fragrant spring flowers, covering the hills and roadsides with fluttering white petals. There are more than 300 members of the *Prunus* genus, along with almonds, cherries, apricots, peaches, and nectarines. When harvesting the blooms to use, remove as much of the stem as possible, as plum stems, twigs, and leaves, like almonds or apple seeds, contain toxic cyanogenic compounds. Harvest the flowers in the morning, as soon as possible after opening, or while they are still closed in the bud, nearly open; this will impart the strongest fragrance. Wild plum flowers make incredibly delicious and floral desserts, jams, and drinks. Wild plum will spread and grow quite easily when it is introduced, so much so that it is considered an invasive in some places in the world.

**YELLOW DOCK SEEDS, *Rumex crispus*:** Yellow dock and other species in the *Rumex* genus of plants have a long history of use by humans. In Silkeborg, Denmark, a "bog body" was discovered in the 1950s of a well-preserved human more than 2,300 years old, who had had a last meal of porridge made from a yellow dock relative.

Yellow dock is also closely related to buckwheat, and the seeds can be lightly toasted and ground into a gluten-free flour that tastes quite similar. This makes for a great winter or fall forage when most other plants have vanished. The seeds come off the stalk easily once they're dry; several cups of seed can be collected in minutes. Yellow dock is often considered an invasive or weed plant, so harvest away and enjoy its seeds in crackers, cookies, and other baked goods.

## INGREDIENT SOURCES

The following organizations and sites are my favorite places to source ingredients if I can't forage or grow them myself.

1. **MOUNTAIN ROSE HERBS**
   (mountainroseherbs.com)
   Bulk herbs, flowers, seaweed, mushrooms, and spices

2. **ANIMA MUNDI HERBS**
   (animamundiherbals.com)
   Specialty herbs and formulas, fine flower and mushroom powders

3. **NUTS DOT COM**
   (nuts.com)
   Organic bulk nuts and seeds, organic flours and sweeteners, dried porcini and other mushrooms

4. **FRONTIER HERBS**
   (www.frontiercoop.com)
   Organic bulk herbs

5. **ETSY**
   (etsy.com)
   Herbs and specialty goods

6. **FORAGED MARKET**
   (www.foraged.com)
   Foraged plants, mushrooms, and fruits

7. **FARMERS' MARKETS**
   Farmers' markets sometimes have foraged plants, such as nettles and lambsquarters, along with all kinds of herbs, edible flowers, and other specialty items. It is always great to get to know your local farmers.

8. **AN BEAN FEASA**
   (www.anbeanfeasa.com)
   Seaweeds, herbs, and other offerings from the west coast of Ireland

9. **ROOT AND BONES**
   (www.rootandbones.com)
   Flower, mushroom, and herb powders with an emphasis on Chinese Traditional Medicine

10. **GOOGLE**
    Just searching in your local area or region can be fruitful; there are local farms and flower, mushroom, and herb growers who may be right down the road. I have found so many people this way.

11. **NEIGHBORS**
    Talk to your neighbors, friends, and community. Ask people whether they have plants to share or offer to "weed" their garden for dandelions or purslane. People are often really happy to share and learn about what you're doing. Offer to bring them some of what you make in exchange for a basket of plants.

# SPRING

# DANDELION PAKORAS
# WITH TAMARIND SAUCE

**SERVES 4**

Pakoras are a lightly fried, traditional Indian street food that are often made in spring with the first fresh vegetables. I start dreaming about this meal when the ground begins to thaw. As soon as the dandelions come up, this is my first celebratory meal of spring with crispy, delicious, and slightly bitter dandelions dipped in a sweet and spiced tamarind sauce.

❀ **FORAGER'S NOTE**  For this recipe, harvest the bottom of the dandelion plant, cutting close to the ground, including leaves, a few unopened buds, and the freshly bloomed flowers.

» **SIMPLE SWAP**  If you do not have dandelions, try using spring onions or thin slices of regular onion in their place.

6 to 12 dandelion plants

¾ cup garbanzo bean flour

½ teaspoon salt

2 teaspoons turmeric powder

½ cup water

3 tablespoons coconut oil or high-heat oil

Tamarind Sauce (recipe follows), for serving

Rinse the dandelions and pat them dry.

Whisk together the flour, salt, turmeric, and water in a medium bowl until smooth. Add more water as needed, a tablespoon at a time, to get a consistency like heavy whipping cream.

Heat the oil in a large skillet or heavy-bottomed pan over medium-low heat. Dip the dandelions, one at a time, into the batter, coating completely and dragging them along the side of the bowl to remove excess batter. Carefully place the battered dandelions, one at a time, in the hot oil. As the batter starts to look dry and cooked on top, flip the entire plant over and cook on the other side for 3 to 5 minutes. They should be golden on both sides.

Set the cooked dandelions on a paper towel–lined plate and serve with the tamarind sauce.

# TAMARIND SAUCE/CHUTNEY

**SERVES 4**

¼ teaspoon fennel seeds

½ teaspoon cumin seeds

1 cup water

½ cup coconut sugar

1 tablespoon tamarind paste

1 teaspoon salt

1 teaspoon ground ginger

Pinch of cayenne pepper

Heat a small skillet over medium heat and lightly toast the fennel seeds until golden and they release a fragrant scent. Grind the seeds in a grinder or with a mortar and pestle.

Combine the ground seeds with all the remaining ingredients in a saucepan and heat over medium heat. Whisk for 10 to 15 minutes, or until thickened. Strain through a mesh sieve and serve with the dandelion pakoras.

# NETTLE & MUSHROOM PÂTÉ ROLLED IN FLOWERS

## SERVES 10 TO 12

This is one of my favorite spring recipes, a rich and green umami pâté to support the transition into the busyness of the season. Awakening the brain and body, attuning us to the greening world outside, spring nettles are used for the adrenals, for the libido, for boosting energy, and for alleviating hay fever and spring allergies. With the addition of lion's mane mushrooms, this plant-based pâté is perfect with crackers, toast, or veggies; and, rolled in flowers, makes a beautiful appetizer or snack.

✤ **FORAGER'S NOTE**  Use gloves to remove nettle leaves from their woody stems to avoid being stung. Harvest only the tops of the nettles, leaving the rest to continue growing.

» **SIMPLE SWAPS**  Use any mushrooms you have available, and if you can't find nettles, use baby spinach or another green of your choice instead.

½ cup cashew pieces

4 to 5 cups fresh nettle leaves

⅔ cup plus 1 tablespoon olive oil, plus more if needed

½ medium yellow onion, chopped

1½ cups fresh lion's mane mushrooms, chopped loosely

½ cup shiitake mushrooms, chopped

½ cup sunflower seeds

2 green garlic stalks with garlic clove, chopped, or 2 large garlic cloves, chopped

1 to 2 teaspoons sea salt, or more to taste

Dried edible flowers or seeds, such as rose petals, calendula, violas, poppy seeds, nettle seeds, or sesame seeds (optional)

Soak the cashews overnight in cool water, or boil enough water to cover them and soak in the hot water for 20 minutes. Drain the cashews and set them aside in a blender.

Bring a pot of salted water to a boil and place the nettle leaves in the water. Cook for 1 minute, then quickly drain and run cold water over the leaves to stop them from cooking.

Heat the tablespoon of olive oil in a large skillet over medium heat. Add the onion, stirring until it becomes translucent. Add the mushrooms to the skillet and sauté until they are softened and starting to brown slightly. You may need to add more olive oil if they are a "drier" mushroom, such as lion's mane. Turn off the heat and add the mixture to the blender that contains the cashews.

In another, dry skillet, quickly toast the sunflower seeds until they are slightly golden and begin to release their scent. Add to the blender along with the garlic, sea salt, and remaining ⅔ cup of olive oil.

Blend until the consistency is very smooth but still thick like a pâté. Add more olive oil if the mixture is too thick, 1 teaspoon at a time, but not too much or it will get runny and taste too much of oil.

Spread the mixture in a large bowl and place in the freezer for 10 minutes so it becomes solid enough to roll into balls. If you don't want to roll it out, scoop the mixture into small Pyrex dishes or mini Bundt pans for a beautiful shape and refrigerate for 2 hours.

Prepare separate small bowls with a few tablespoons of each flower or seed you plan to roll your pâté balls in, and prepare a small bowl of water and oil to dip your fingers in between rolling. Dip your fingers in the water. Using a spoon, scoop about 1½ tablespoons of mixture into your hand and roll it into a ball. Roll the ball in flowers or seeds and place on a plate. Repeat until you're done with the whole mixture. Refrigerate for 20 minutes to 2 hours before serving. You can freeze large batches of this pâté for up to 3 months and let them warm to room temperature before serving. Serve the pâté balls with crackers, breads, or fresh vegetables.

# CREAMY NETTLE &
# LEMON BALM HUMMUS

**MAKES 4 TO 6 SERVINGS**

Lemon balm and nettle are perfect herbs to add to this creamy, spring green hummus. This is a perfect recipe to go with spring veggies, Yellow Dock & Nettle Seed Crackers (page 190) or chips. Nettles contain loads of vitamins and minerals, protein, and calcium; and lemon balm is a gentle nervine that adds a light citrus flavor.

❀ **FORAGER'S NOTE** Nettles must be harvested with gloves to avoid stings, and young spring nettles are less likely to sting than nettles that are further along in their growth in summer or fall.

» **SIMPLE SWAP** Spring spinach, kale, or chard will work in place of the nettles.

¼ cup fresh nettles

¼ cup fresh lemon balm

One 15-ounce can chickpeas, liquid reserved, or cook your own

¼ cup liquid from the chickpeas, or more as needed

¼ cup tahini

2 tablespoons freshly squeezed lemon juice

¼ cup olive oil, plus more for serving

½ teaspoon salt, more to taste

1 to 2 garlic cloves

1 teaspoon ground cumin

¼ teaspoon dried oregano

Bring water to a boil in a small pot. Add the nettles and lemon balm and blanch them for about 10 seconds. Drain and immediately cool them under cold running water. Squeeze them out, then add them to a high-speed blender. Add all the remaining ingredients on top and blend until smooth and creamy!

Taste and add more salt, or more liquid from the chickpeas for an even smoother hummus. Serve in a bowl with a drizzle of olive oil, a sprinkle of paprika or sumac, and edible flowers and/or nettle seeds.

# SNOW PEA WARM SALAD WITH BLACK LOCUST FLOWERS

**SERVES 4**

Black locust flowers are a foraged treat that come from the blooming honey-sweet stands of black locust trees this time of year. The scent is intoxicating, and the flavor is sweet and crunchy. The flowers are said to be soothing for the nervous system, may relieve migraines and joint pain, and may be helpful for the digestive system. This salad is a combination of crisp and fresh ingredients, including slightly warmed and sautéed mushrooms and fresh peas—a perfect balance for this spring meal.

❧ **FORAGER'S NOTE** The flowers are the only edible part of the tree; everything else is toxic from the bark to the seed pods, so it is essential to harvest and use only the flowers.

» **SIMPLE SWAP** This salad can be made without the flowers, if they are not available where you live, or feel free to substitute another flower or to add more cucumber or peas.

3 to 4 tablespoons olive oil

3 garlic cloves, chopped finely

3 cups shiitake mushrooms, diced

1 teaspoon salt, more to taste

2½ to 3 cups snow peas, any variety (the peas pictured are a purple variety)

1 tablespoon finely chopped fresh thyme

3 tablespoons finely chopped fresh chives

2 tablespoons diced preserved lemon

1 cup sliced cucumber, cut into thin rounds and quartered

1 cup black locust flowers

Heat 1 tablespoon of the olive oil in a large skillet over medium heat. Add the garlic, stirring until it releases its scent and begins to get golden. Add the shiitake mushrooms, let them release any liquid and then absorb it, and then add ½ teaspoon of the salt. Cook, stirring, until the mushrooms get golden and crispy, adding more oil if needed. Add the peas and 1 teaspoon of the thyme on top of the mushrooms, stir, and cover with a lid. Transfer the mixture to a large bowl.

Mix together the remaining 2 teaspoons of thyme, the chives, the preserved lemon, and 2 to 3 tablespoons of olive oil in a small bowl. Add the fresh cucumbers to the large bowl, dress the salad with the oil and lemon mixture, and scatter the flowers on top. Eat immediately.

# LAND-DWELLER
# SEAWEED SALAD

**SERVES 4**

This salad is an ode to the sea using a plant called minutina, also known as herba stella or buckshorn plantain, which reminds me of mineral-rich seaweeds. I love being by the ocean, and grew up near the water, although I have lived in the high desert and mountains for most of my adult life. I find that living away from the water now, I gravitate toward plants and food that evoke the sea. Minutina has a slightly nutty flavor, is endemic to Italy and Africa, and now grows all over the world. Medicinally, it is cooling and soothing, has been used as a febrifuge, a diuretic, and as a skin-healing plant. A bit of seaweed is added to the mix for good measure, but ultimately this dish is made to evoke the briny waters wherever you may dwell. This is the perfect salad to serve alongside Seasonal Petal Rolls (page 97) or with Sizzling Garlic & Chili Noodles (page 58).

» **SIMPLE SWAPS**  You can substitute black kale for the minutina leaves, and replace the ume vinegar with more lemon juice and sea salt to taste.

¼ cup dried arame, wakame, or hijiki seaweed

6 cups fresh minutina leaves or kale, stripped off the ribs and cut lengthwise into thin strips

1 tablespoon black sesame seeds, plus more to taste

1 tablespoon white sesame seeds, plus more to taste

1 to 2 tablespoons soy sauce, or to taste

1 tablespoon ume plum vinegar

1 teaspoon freshly squeezed lemon juice

3 tablespoons toasted sesame oil

Sea salt

Soak your preferred seaweed in water until fully rehydrated, about 7 minutes. Drain, then set aside.

Boil 6 to 8 quarts of water in a large pot, adding ⅛ to ¼ cup of sea salt, making it taste nearly like the sea. Stir in the minutina and blanch for 3 to 5 minutes. The leaves should be soft but not mushy. For kale, blanch for only about a minute. Drain the greens and plunge them into an ice bath to stop them from cooking. Drain again and squeeze the greens out. Mix the blanched greens and seaweed together in a medium bowl.

Toast the white and black sesame seeds together in a small, dry skillet over low heat, stirring constantly, until they release their scent, 3 to 5 minutes. Remove from the heat and set aside. Whisk together the soy sauce, ume plum vinegar, lemon juice, and sesame oil in a small bowl. Pour the soy sauce mixture over the greens and mix well, adding sea salt to taste.

Top with the toasted sesame seeds, cover, and place in the refrigerator to marinate for at least an hour before serving.

# FORAGED GREENS TABBOULEH SALAD

**MAKES 3 TO 4 CUPS**

This refreshing salad is a burst of herby flavor, perfect with the hummus on page 44 or as a spring side dish. Tabbouleh salad originated in Lebanon, where it is traditionally made with wild greens that come up in spring and early summer. Often it is prepared with bulgur wheat, but in some regions is made grain-free, like this version. In spring, wild plants can act as natural digestives, detoxifying tonics, and adrenal support. They are a great addition to our diet, supporting our body in waking up as we transition into warmer months.

» **SIMPLE SWAP** Use 1 to 2 tablespoons of freshly squeezed lemon juice if you do not have preserved lemons.

1½ cups dandelion leaves

1½ cups fresh parsley

¼ cup fresh mint leaves

¾ cup hemp seeds

3 to 5 tablespoons extra-virgin olive oil

2 tablespoons diced preserved lemon

Freshly squeezed lemon juice

Salt and freshly ground black pepper

Finely chop the dandelion leaves, parsley, and mint or pulse them in a food processor, and transfer them to a medium bowl. Stir in the hemp seeds.

Whisk together the olive oil, preserved lemon, a squeeze of lemon juice, and salt and pepper to taste in a small bowl. Pour the lemon-and-oil mixture over the greens and hemp seeds, and mix well. Chill in a covered bowl in the refrigerator for 2 hours or more, then serve.

# NETTLE & LOVAGE POTATO SOUP WITH ROASTED WILD ASPARAGUS & CHIVE FLOWER

**SERVES 6**

Nettles are far and away my favorite plant, and this is a soup for the early spring days, warming and tonifying, a taste of the verdant new growth of the season. Nettles contain all the essential amino acids, vitamins A, C, K, and B vitamins, iron, calcium, and protein, among many other nutrients. Nettles are used as a diuretic and adrenal tonic plant, and to awaken and energize the body. Nettle soup has been eaten for thousands of years, with some suggesting its origin in Britain during the Bronze Age. The recipe varies from household to household and in different regions, but there is generally a base of new potatoes and onion paired with nettles and broth, making for a spoonful of spring in every bite. Including spring asparagus, lovage, and sprinkles of spring onion and edible flowers is a beautiful addition, but not necessary for the recipe. Enjoy while the rain falls with a slice of cornbread, or outside while the spring sun warms your skin.

✸ **FORAGER'S NOTES** When harvesting nettles, wear sturdy gloves unless you want to be stung, which is a healing practice in itself but definitely not for everyone. Use scissors to cut just the tops of the plants, taking only the first four or so leaves. If you have a patch you are tending, the leaves will continue to grow and can be harvested again in fall when the weather cools down. Remember to harvest ethically, taking only what is needed from a healthy patch, leaving plenty to go to seed.

» **SIMPLE SWAP** You can substitute spinach or any dark leafy spring green for nettles in this recipe, but it will have a different texture. Leave out the lovage if you don't have it.

*continued* »

2 tablespoons olive oil

1 yellow onion, chopped

2 garlic cloves, chopped finely

3 cups peeled, chopped potatoes
(cut into small chunks)

8 cups vegetable broth or water

8 cups loosely packed nettles

2 tablespoons fresh lovage, or 1
teaspoon dried

1 bunch of asparagus,
ends trimmed

Salt

½ cup chopped spring onion

Edible flowers (such as dandelion
petals, nasturtium, or violets),
for topping (optional)

Sour cream, yogurt, or
crème fraîche of your
choice (optional)

Heat 1 tablespoon of the olive oil in a large, heavy-bottomed pot over medium heat. Add the onion and sauté until translucent. Add the garlic and cook for just a minute longer, or until the garlic releases its scent.

Add the potatoes and broth to the pot and stir everything together. Lower the heat to a simmer, cover, and cook for about 10 minutes, or until the potatoes are soft enough to be easily pricked with a fork. Stir in the nettles and simmer for 4 to 5 minutes longer. Remove from the heat and stir in the lovage.

Using a handheld blender, blend the soup until smooth and creamy. Alternatively, working in batches, blend the soup in a standard blender, returning it to the pot when fully blended.

Heat the remaining oil in a large skillet over high heat until shimmering. Carefully add the asparagus in a single layer across the skillet; the oil may pop and sizzle, so make sure to protect yourself as you add the asparagus. Cook the asparagus quickly, letting it get lightly browned on one side, about 5 minutes. Sprinkle with salt to taste and turn off the heat; the texture of the asparagus should be slightly crisp and fresh, but cooked.

To serve, ladle the soup into bowls and top with the asparagus, spring onions, and flowers. Add a spoonful of sour cream, yogurt, or crème fraîche (if using) to the top, for a more velvety consistency.

# SCALLION PANCAKES WITH SPRING GREENS & MUSHROOMS

**SERVES 4**

Scallion pancakes are a perfect blend of savory light onion flavor and crispy, chewy texture. I was dreaming of my favorite Chinese restaurant that we frequented when I was a kid and made these with all the fresh growing plants of spring. They are made in a mostly traditional Chinese street style, but they are gluten-free and include mushrooms and foraged greens. This can be made with almost anything you have on hand and is perfect for the abundant spring season.

» **SIMPLE SWAPS** Use a combination of greens and add the mushrooms or use traditional scallions.

### DIPPING SAUCE (OPTIONAL)
2 tablespoons soy sauce

2 tablespoons rice vinegar

2 teaspoons chopped scallion

### PANCAKES
2 cups scallion

1½ cups nettles, lambsquarters, dandelion greens, mallow leaves, violet leaves, or other spring greens

½ cup assorted mushrooms

2 cups cassava flour

¼ cup arrowroot starch or tapioca starch

1 teaspoon salt, plus more for sprinkling

1¼ cups boiling water

1 tablespoon sesame oil, plus more for brushing

Prepare the dipping sauce (if using): Mix all the sauce ingredients together in a small bowl and set aside.

Prepare the pancakes: If using nettles, you can blanch them in boiling water for 1 to 2 minutes and then rinse them in cold water before continuing. Roughly chop the scallion, nettles or other greens, and mushrooms together, popping the mixture into a food processor, and pulsing just a few times. Set the mixture aside.

Combine the tapioca flour, arrowroot flour, and salt in a large bowl. Pour in the boiling hot water; mix with a metal spoon and then your hands until the dough is smooth but not sticky. If it is really sticky, add a sprinkle of arrowroot starch and mix again until it is smooth. You really want this dough to be smooth, not dry or cracking.

Divide the dough into eight equal-size balls. Place the balls in a bowl and cover with a clean, damp cloth to ensure they do not dry out as you are rolling. Between two pieces of parchment paper, roll out the first ball evenly until it is very thin, about ⅛ inch thick. Paint the dough with sesame oil, sprinkle with a little salt, and spread 3 to 4 tablespoons of the greens mixture over the center of the pancake. Roll the pancake in on itself so you have

a fairly tight roll. Then, wrap that roll around itself as if you are rolling up a cinnamon roll, so it looks like a snail shell or spiral. Using the rolling pin again, roll out the spiral into a ¼-inch-thick disk. Repeat with each of your dough balls.

Heat the 1 tablespoon of sesame oil in a skillet over medium heat, and cook one pancake at a time on one side until golden brown, 3 to 5 minutes, then brush more oil on the uncooked side and flip it over to cook for 3 to 5 minutes. Transfer the pancakes to a plate when they are done. Once all the pancakes have been cooked, serve with the dipping sauce or eat the pancakes on their own. These are best eaten as you make them, so that they're fresh and crispy, but I also love to fry up leftover pancakes and eat them for breakfast.

## To make a colorful socca, add these ingredients:

RED  ¼ cup of beet juice substituted for ¼ cup of the water.

BLUE  2 teaspoons of blue spirulina plus 1 teaspoon of butterfly pea flower powder whisked into the 1 cup of flour. If you don't have both of these ingredients, you can use 1 tablespoon of either one.

GREEN  2 tablespoons of powdered nettles plus 2 dropperfuls of liquid chlorophyll stirred into the batter.

YELLOW  2 teaspoons turmeric powder plus 2 teaspoons of yellow curry powder stirred into the batter.

# MINI RAINBOW SOCCA (SAVORY PANCAKES) WITH HERBS & MUSHROOMS

**SERVES 4 TO 8 AS ONE 10-INCH SOCCA, OR TWO SMALL SOCCA**

Socca is a golden and delicious street food from Nice, France, with versions originating in Italy under the name "farinata" or "torta de ceci." Traditionally, socca would be cooked over an open fire or grill in giant pans, but it works great on the stovetop and in an oven. The first socca I made years ago was an experiment of bright green kale and basil from my garden, and I was inspired to add different colors and plants to the batter to make a palette of color and flavor that echoes spring. These can be as simple as you have time for, or as complex as you can dream. I like to double or triple the base recipe and make each socca unique.

1 cup garbanzo bean flour

1 teaspoon sea salt

Freshly ground black pepper

1 cup water

6 tablespoons olive oil, plus more for brushing and oiling

Fresh or dried herbs, edible flowers, mushrooms, cherry tomatoes, or sun-dried tomatoes (optional)

Yogurt of your choice or Salsa Rioja (page 96), for serving

Preheat the oven to 475° or 500°F. Place a rack almost as high as it goes in the oven and put a cast-iron skillet on this rack in the oven to warm. If you are making one large socca, make sure your skillet is at least 10 inches in diameter.

To make the batter, whisk or blend the garbanzo bean flour, salt, pepper, water, and 3 tablespoons of the olive oil in a medium bowl until the batter is smooth like a thickened heavy cream.

Remove the skillet from the oven and add the remaining olive oil, or enough to completely coat it, to the bottom of the pan. If you are making one large socca, pour in the entire batter. If you are making smaller, colorful socca, pour in approximately one-third of the mixture at a time. Quickly add any toppings, flowers, herbs, or mushrooms to the top of the socca. You can arrange them in a design, if you wish. Then, place the pan in the oven and bake for 7 to 10 minutes, checking on the socca at the end of 7 minutes to see when it gets solid. Once the socca looks solid, remove it from the oven and quickly brush the top with olive oil before putting it back in the oven for just a few more minutes, until the edges begin to get crisp and golden brown.

Remove the socca from the oven and serve with yogurt or Salsa Rioja, or eat with a crisp salad.

# SIZZLING GARLIC & CHILI NOODLES WITH FORAGED GREENS

**SERVES 2 TO 4**

This is an easy noodle recipe with a mouthwatering combination of flavors. This was inspired by some of the quick noodle dishes I picked up when I went to Thailand many years ago and spent time with a chef there, learning to navigate the bustling fresh markets and cook with the balance of flavors and ingredients that Thai cooking embodies. Food became infinitely more exciting with umami, sour, sweet, and spicy flavor, all perfectly balanced. This recipe works great with gluten-free ramen noodles, but feel free to use any noodles or greens you have available or enjoy. This meal is delicious with Redbud Flower "Capers" (page 220) on top, and a side of Cucumber, Cucamelon & Purslane Salad (page 89), or Land-Dweller Seaweed Salad (page 48).

## SAUCE
2 teaspoons soy sauce

1 tablespoon cider vinegar, plant-infused vinegar, black vinegar, or lime juice

2 teaspoons coconut aminos

## NOODLES
8 to 10 ounces ramen noodles, cooked per package instructions

½ cup finely chopped foraged spring greens, such as dandelion, nettles, mallow, or lambsquarters

3 to 4 garlic cloves, chopped finely or crushed

1 to 2 tablespoons chili powder; I love the Korean chili blend called gochugaru

¼ cup finely chopped spring onions

¼ cup sesame or avocado oil

Salt

2 tablespoons mixed white and black sesame seeds, for topping

Make the sauce: Mix together the soy sauce, vinegar, and coconut aminos in a small bowl and set aside.

Make the noodles: Have your cooked noodles ready and set aside. Combine the spring greens, garlic, chili powder, and spring onions in a large, heat-safe bowl. Heat the oil in a small skillet until wavy and very hot. You can test the oil by putting a little bit of spring onion in the pan to see whether it sizzles immediately. As soon as the oil is hot enough, pour it over the greens mixture and quickly whisk it in with a fork. Add the noodles to the bowl and quickly mix everything together, tossing well to coat.

Add salt to taste, add protein if you like, and top with the sesame seeds to serve.

# LEMON BALM, NETTLE & GREEN OLIVE PASTA WITH PINE NUTS

**SERVES 4**

Lemon balm has a floral and slightly citrus flavor that carries through in this herbaceous sauce. It is one of my favorite spring herbs to add to both sweet and savory meals with its gentle yet powerful medicinal properties. It can aid in digestion, soothe the nervous system, help with insomnia, and is known to be an excellent support for emotional well-being. Adding the olives gives the sauce more body and an almost creamy texture. This recipe freezes so well, and it will stay good in the refrigerator for about five days.

» SIMPLE SWAP  This recipe can be made with regular garlic cloves and basil in place of green garlic and lemon balm.

10 to 12 ounces uncooked pasta; I love fusilli for this recipe

¾ cup fresh lemon balm

½ cup nettles

¾ cup olives, different varieties and without pits (example: ¼ cup Castelvetrano and ½ cup Kalamata)

½ teaspoon fresh oregano

1 to 2 green garlic bulbs with 2 inches of the green stems, or 1 to 2 garlic cloves, smashed, plus more to taste

1 teaspoon freshly squeezed lemon juice

¼ teaspoon salt, more to taste

Grated rind of ¼ lemon

3 tablespoons olive oil, or to taste

Optional toppings: 2 tablespoons toasted pine nuts, 2 tablespoons chopped sun-dried tomatoes, chopped fresh basil

Cook the pasta in well-salted water according to the package directions, until al dente. While the pasta is cooking, bring water to a boil in a small pot and blanch the nettles and lemon balm for 10 seconds. Drain and immediately plunge them into cold water to stop them from cooking. Squeeze them out and then add them to a food processor with your olives, oregano, garlic, lemon juice, all but ¼ teaspoon of the lemon zest, and the olive oil. Blend until smooth. Taste and add more salt or olive oil, if needed.

Mix about half of the sauce into your cooked pasta. Add the reserved lemon rind and your preferred toppings and serve with a salad or cooked greens, sautéed mushrooms, or protein of your choice. Store the rest of the sauce in the refrigerator or freezer, and thaw 30 minutes before using.

# SPRING ONIGIRI WITH CRISPY MUSHROOMS

**SERVES 4**

Onigiri is a simple yet flavorful Japanese snack or meal made of short-grain rice and traditionally stuffed with pickled ume plums, cured fish, or vegetables. Onigiri has been eaten for hundreds of years, originally shaped into triangles by Shintoist travelers, offering protection and honoring the form of the sacred mountains they journeyed through.

I have always loved onigiri. These are colored with butterfly pea flowers and filled with roasted winter squash and fermented radish. Experiment with a combination of vegetables, mushrooms, or protein that you like. The mild-tasting ground butterfly pea flowers turn the rice a brilliant blue and create a beautiful contrast with the orange squash. Onigiri can be made in advance, wrapped in plastic or beeswax wrap, and stored for up to five days in the refrigerator. Wrap with nori strips before serving.

2 cups uncooked sushi rice or other short-grain rice

2 tablespoons butterfly pea flowers, or 1 tablespoon pea flower powder

1 small winter squash (roughly 16 to 24 ounces), such as pumpkin, butternut, or acorn, halved and seeded

Olive oil for brushing

Salt

1 to 2 cups oyster or enoki mushrooms

1 to 2 tablespoons gomasio or Forager's Everything Salt Blend (page 229; optional)

Sea salt (optional)

2 to 3 sheets nori seaweed

¼ cup Lacto-Fermented Purple Daikon Radish (page 231)

1 tablespoon olive oil

Prepare the rice as directed on the package, using a ratio of 1 cup of water for every cup of rice, and stirring the butterfly pea flowers or powder into the cooking water. Set the rice aside once it has cooked.

While the rice is cooking, line a baking sheet with parchment paper and preheat the oven to 425°F. Rub olive oil on the outside and the inside of your squash halves and place them, cut side down, on the prepared baking sheet. Cut off and discard the bottoms or woody stems from the mushrooms, leaving several whole if they are small. Brush them with olive oil and sprinkle them with salt. Place them on the baking sheet with the squash.

Bake the vegetables for 25 to 30 minutes, checking at about 10 minutes to make sure your mushrooms are browning. Remove the mushrooms when they are golden and slightly crisp, 10 to 15 minutes depending on the size of the mushrooms, and set them aside. Remove the squash after 25 to 30 minutes, or when it begins to soften. Once cool enough to handle, scoop out the squash from its skin and place in a bowl.

Let the rice cool enough that it is still slightly warm but easy to handle, which will make it easiest for you to shape your rice

balls. Add the gomasio or salt blend (if using) to the rice and if not using either, add roughly ½ teaspoon of sea salt to the rice, stirring well to incorporate.

Prepare a bowl of water to dip your fingers into as you mold the rice. Cut the nori into 2-by-6-inch rectangular strips, then set the strips aside. Most nori sheets have perforated lines in them already, and you can follow them or cut your own.

Scoop about 3 tablespoons of rice into your hand and mold it into a ball. Then, form it into a round-edged triangle. Use your thumb to indent the middle of the triangle, and place a little spoonful of the squash and fermented daikon in the center. Cover the opening with a little more rice to seal in your filling. Repeat this process until you run out of rice. If you are eating your rice balls right away, wrap them each with one strip of nori, or save them for later by wrapping them in plastic or beeswax wrap and refrigerating. Serve with the crispy mushrooms, and if you want, vegetable broth with a spoonful of miso, and more fermented vegetables on the side.

# LILAC ICE POPS

**MAKES 4 POPS**

Lilac flowers waft clouds of fragrance through open windows this time of year; these ice pops share in the color and essence of this favorite spring bloom. Lilac products were one of the first things I made as a culinary herbalist. My little adobe house in New Mexico was shrouded in purple blooms, and I made lilac and vanilla bean jelly to sell. Lilacs love a gentle treatment to impart their scent and flavor without becoming bitter. The ice pops are subtle, but the flower essence is there. Savor these ephemeral beauties on a hot day when the heady scent of lilacs is floating in on the breeze.

✤ **FORAGER'S NOTE** Harvest your lilacs in the morning after the dew has dried; make an offering, a thank-you, for their blooms.

1 cup lilac blossoms, removed from their stems, plus more for freezing

1 quart spring water, at room temperature

3 tablespoons honey or cane sugar, or more to taste

Zest of ½ small grapefruit

1 tablespoon freshly squeezed grapefruit juice

¼ teaspoon butterfly pea flower powder

Make sure you completely remove the lilac flowers from the stems and green bits, as these can be quite bitter. Place the lilac blooms in a quart-size mason jar. Cover them with room-temperature spring water up to the shoulder of the jar. Cover with a lid before placing in the refrigerator overnight or for 24 hours.

Ready four ice pop molds and add a few lilac flowers to each mold. Mix together the honey and the grapefruit zest and juice in a small bowl. Remove the lilac water from the fridge. The water should have a strong lilac scent now. Strain the liquid into a bowl, giving the flowers a squeeze as you strain them. Discard the squeezed flowers. Pour the lilac water back into the jar, whisk in the butterfly pea powder, and stir in the honey mixture.

Pour the liquid into the prepared ice pop molds. Freeze the ice pops until they are set, and enjoy with your inner child.

# SPRUCE TIP ICE POPS

## MAKES 4 TO 6 POPS DEPENDING ON MOLD SIZE

I love the citrus flavor of spruce and fir tips and look forward to collecting the emergent, glowing green tips in the spring and summer months. Aside from being extremely delicious, spruce and fir syrups are packed with vitamin C, terpenes, and other beneficial compounds, making them a support for colds and congestion, and for soothing sore throats. Even with the heating that is necessary, you will still retain many of the benefits. I love to keep the syrup from this recipe on hand for winter colds and sore throats; you can add it to tea, or make ice pops as I do here.

I do not generally use sugar in my recipes except to make alcoholic brews or syrups. I often prefer honey for its medicinal uses, including its antibacterial and antiviral properties. Honey can soothe sore throats and respiratory irritation. Sugar will show off the full flavor of the spruce or fir tips more than honey, and I enjoy both; just make sure the sugar is completely dissolved.

✻ FORAGER'S NOTES  Spruce, fir, or pine are amazing trees to connect with and gather tips from in small amounts. Any edible conifer will work for these, but make sure you are not harvesting from a yew tree or any other toxic or poisonous conifer. Never remove too many fresh tips from any single tree, as this is the new growth. When harvesting in winter or fall, the tips will not be as bright green and the flavor will differ. As the weather gets colder, conifers may produce larger amounts of vitamin C, in addition to pathogen-fighting properties.

2 cups honey or raw sugar

2 cups water

2 cups spruce or fir tips

1 tablespoon freshly squeezed lemon juice

4 to 6 dropperfuls of concentrate of chlorophyll made from nettles or alfalfa (optional)

Water or juice of your choice (I recommend grapefruit juice or lemonade)

Combine the honey and water in a medium saucepan over medium heat and bring to a boil, then turn off the heat. Stir in the spruce tips and cover with a heavy lid for 2 to 8 hours, or overnight. Strain through a fine-mesh sieve, pressing the tips with the back of a large spoon and reserving the syrup. You can keep this syrup refrigerated for up to a month, or freeze into ice pops, ice cubes, or small jars for use all year-round.

Ready your ice pop molds and pour 2 to 3 tablespoons of syrup into each mold. Then, add a squeeze of lemon juice and a dropperful of chlorophyll to each, fill the rest up of each mold with water or juice of your choice, and freeze. I love to keep a sealed container of these spruce pops in the freezer.

# NETTLE & GINGER
# ROOT ICE CREAM

**SERVES 4 TO 6**

Nettle and ginger combine perfectly with a base of slightly tart green apple for a refreshing and vibrant dessert. It is light and creamy and comes together quickly in a blender. This ice cream is made with dried and powdered nettle leaf, so you can make it anywhere and anytime. I like to serve this ice cream with Honey Sesame Caramels (page 70), but you can easily enjoy it on its own.

3 to 4 green apples, cored and chopped loosely

⅓ cup coconut cream (scoop the top layer off a can of full-fat coconut milk)

1 teaspoon pure vanilla extract

¼ cup pure maple syrup, honey, or sweetener of your choice

1 to 2 teaspoons grated fresh ginger

Pinch of sea salt

2 to 4 dropperfuls of liquid chlorophyll

1 tablespoon dried nettles

Combine all the ingredients, except the dried nettles, in a blender. Place the dried nettles in a clean coffee or spice grinder, grind thoroughly, then use a fine-mesh sieve or tea strainer to sift the nettles into the mixture in the blender; they should be a fine powder. Discard any leftover chunky bits.

Blend everything on high speed until creamy and smooth. Chill in the refrigerator until cool, 10 to 20 minutes. Pour into an ice-cream maker and let it run for about 10 minutes, or until the mixture is thick and frozen. Alternatively, you can pour the mixture into a container and place it in the freezer, mixing every 15 minutes until it has a soft yet frozen consistency.

When the ice cream is perfectly smooth, spoon it into bowls and enjoy!

# HONEY SESAME CARAMELS

**SERVES 4 TO 6**

A combination of honey and toasted sesame with ginger and rose—these caramels are the perfect companions to Nettle & Ginger Root Ice Cream (page 69). But they are also divine treats in their own right. This is a recipe that is done when it looks and feels done, and there is a lot of room for variation. The honey can burn, so it must be watched carefully. No matter how you prefer the texture of your caramels, these are delicious when really chewy or completely hard and crisp.

1 tablespoon white sesame seeds

1 tablespoon black sesame seeds

2 tablespoons honey

⅛ teaspoon ginger powder

Generous pinch of salt

⅛ teaspoon rose powder (optional)

Line a baking sheet with parchment paper. Heat a small skillet over medium heat. Add the sesame seeds and dry toast them until they begin to become fragrant, stirring frequently. When the seeds are toasted, add the honey to the pan and start to whisk. The honey will bubble up in larger bubbles, somewhat frothy, and depending on the amount of water it contains, it will have large bubbles for a few minutes.

Keep whisking every 10 seconds or so, until the honey calms down and the mixture begins to get smoother and darker in color. It will look similar to smooth light brown leather. This will take around 10 minutes, depending on the water content of the honey. When it smells like caramel and is smooth with only small bubbles, it is ready.

The honey will be extremely hot at this point, so carefully scoop it, 1 tablespoon at a time, onto your prepared pan, making thin rounds with the liquid, spreading each with the back of a spoon. Alternatively, you can pour it evenly onto the prepared pan in one large spread.

As soon as it is cool enough to touch but still warm, it's ready to handle. If you made thin rounds, roll them with your hands into small fluted shapes. If you made one large piece of caramel, cut it to make shards of the candy. Serve with Nettle & Ginger Root Ice Cream or eat as a rich candy on its own.

# SPRUCE TIP MOCHI ICE CREAM

Spruce tips are an explosion of citrus and forest flavor, the fresh growth that spring represents. Their depth is unparalleled, and infusing them in this creamy base allows their full expression to come through, rounding out the rough edges of conifer terpenes. Mochi originally comes from Japan, but similar pounded rice cakes are found in many countries in the world. In Japan, mochi was a sacred food served at imperial dinners and ceremonies more than 2,000 years ago. Mochi filled with ice cream came about in the 1980s and remains popular to this day.

This ice cream base is my go-to for a dairy-free ice cream, but it can be made with any base, including cream or other dairy.

» **SIMPLE SWAP** If you cannot find spruce, try this with lime zest and vanilla extract. Or try it with another flavor of ice cream that you love. Some of my favorites are mugwort, roasted dandelion root, rose, and lilac.

## ICE CREAM

One 13.5-ounce can full-fat coconut milk (about 1½ cups)

Scant ½ cup honey, maple syrup, or sugar

½ cup spruce tips, plus more to taste

1½ cups raw cashews, soaked in water overnight, or in just-boiled water for 20 minutes

Pinch of sea salt

1 teaspoon vanilla bean paste, or 2 teaspoons pure vanilla extract

Prepare your ice cream: Heat the coconut milk in a medium saucepan over medium heat until it comes to a simmer. If you are using sugar instead of honey or maple syrup, add it to the milk at this point and whisk over low heat until it is completely dissolved. Once your sugar is fully dissolved, add the ½ cup of spruce tips, covering the pan immediately and turning off the heat. Leave the spruce tips to infuse in the milk for 1 hour or overnight.

Drain the soaked cashews completely. Place in a blender. Use a fine-mesh strainer to strain the spruce tips from the milk, squeezing the spruce against the mesh and reserving the milk and spruce. Mince the spruce tips and combine them and the cashews, sea salt, and vanilla paste, plus the honey or maple syrup, if using, in a high-speed blender. Blend until extremely smooth. Taste and add salt or more honey or other sweetener, if needed, and add more spruce if you want a stronger flavor.

*continued »*

### MOCHI

¾ cup sweet or glutinous
  white rice flour or
  mochiko/shiratamako flour

¼ cup maple sugar or granulated
  sugar of your choice

4 dropperfuls of liquid chlorophyll
  or a green food coloring of
  your choice

¾ cup water

½ cup potato starch or cornstarch
  for dusting

Pour into an ice-cream maker and follow the directions for your machine to spin the ice cream until it is thick and frozen. Line a muffin tin with liners and, using an ice-cream scoop, scoop the frozen ice cream into each liner so that the rounded side of the scoop is facing up. Using a standard ice-cream scoop that has a trigger, with a volume of about 2 tablespoons, makes it easier to round the top of the mochi, but any scoop or spoon will work. Once you have 8 to 12 small balls of ice cream, place the tin in the freezer to harden the scoops before you make the mochi.

Make the mochi: Whisk together the rice flour and sugar in a small, heatproof bowl. Add the water and chlorophyll coloring and stir until everything is incorporated. Place a steamer basket (or heatproof lid, upside down) in a 6- to 8-quart saucepan with a heavy lid. You should be able to balance your small bowl level on the basket or inner lid. Fill the bottom of the pot with several inches of water, to below the steamer or inner lid, and place the bowl of mochi mixture on the steamer basket or lid.

For a much faster version of this ice cream, it can be made by blending store-bought vanilla ice cream of your choice with very finely diced spruce needles, about 1 pint of ice cream to 2 tablespoons diced spruce needles; add more or less to taste. It won't be identical in flavor, but will still be delicious and convey the flavor of the forest.

When making this mochi, you must use mochiko, shiratamako, or sweet/glutinous (which is gluten-free) white rice flour. There is no substitute for this; do not use plain white or brown rice flour.

Wrap the outer lid of the pot tightly in a kitchen towel or old, clean cotton T-shirt and place it on top of the pot. This will prevent any condensation from dripping back down into your mochi mixture. Over medium heat, bring the water in the pot to a boil to steam the mochi mixture. After 7 to 8 minutes, uncover the pot and stir the mochi mixture with a spatula. Check your water level and add more water, if needed, still below the steamer or inner lid. Bring the water back to a boil with the outer lid on, and steam for another 8 minutes, or until your mixture looks somewhat translucent.

Lay out parchment paper on a cutting board or other surface small enough that it can be put into your freezer, and dust it heavily with the potato starch. Scoop the sticky mochi mixture onto the board and sprinkle heavily with more potato starch. Using your hands, spread it out to about ½-inch thickness, or roll it out with a well-dusted rolling pin. Place the board in the freezer for 10 minutes, or until the mixture has cooled down significantly but isn't hard.

Pull the mochi from the freezer, dust it and the rolling pin again with potato starch, and roll it to about ¼-inch thickness. Use the lid of a wide mouth or standard mason jar to cut 8 to 12 disks from the mochi. Once they are cut out, you can smash it all together and roll it out again, cutting any remaining circles. Once all the mochi disks are cut, brush off the excess starch with a pastry or clean paintbrush.

Take the ice cream balls from the freezer. Holding a mochi disk in your palm, place an ice cream ball, rounded side down, on top of the disk; this will be the top of the mochi. Fold the mochi up and around the ice cream ball, pinching where it joins until it is completely sealed. Place it, sealed side down, back into the lined muffin tin. Continue until all your mochi disks are filled. Freeze for 3 to 4 hours. Pull the mochi balls out of the freezer 5 minutes before eating, to let them soften slightly.

# LILAC & NETTLE
# ICE-CREAM SANDWICHES

**MAKES 8 LARGE SANDWICHES, 16 LARGE COOKIES, OR 24 SMALLER COOKIES**

This is a lightly sweet dairy-free ice cream that I first made for an inspired plant class given by one of my dearest friends, Rachel, nearly seven years ago; there were reports of transcendent visions and dreams of fairy lands after a nearly silent devouring of the sandwiches. While I can't confirm how true these reports are, I can confirm that this is a delightful spring treat for cooling down as the weather heats up.

Lilac ice cream holds the essence of lilacs, but is not overly floral; it is a perfect fit between two nettle cookies or scooped right into a rolled cone. Lilacs are a lifelong love of mine and favorite medicinal flower, related to the twisting wise old olive trees. In the past, they were rumored to be antiperiodic and antimalaria. This is my daughter Nila's favorite ice cream, so I make a double batch to enjoy all through the month of June. You can also make the ice cream and cookies to enjoy separately!

☙ **FORAGER'S NOTE** Harvest lilacs, and all flowers, in the morning after dew has dried a bit, and before the full heat of the day starts, as they will have a higher water content and the fragrance and flavor will be strongest.

» **SIMPLE SWAP** Use any kind of milk you like to replace the coconut milk.

**LILAC ICE CREAM**

One 13.5-ounce can full-fat coconut milk (roughly 1½ cups)
1 cup lilac flowers, stems and green bits removed
1½ cups raw cashews
1 tablespoon butterfly pea flower powder
Scant ½ cup honey
Pinch of sea salt
2 tablespoons melted refined coconut oil (optional)

Gently warm the coconut milk in a small saucepan over low heat, but do not boil. When the coconut milk is warm, turn off the heat. Add the lilac flowers to the milk, stir, and cover immediately. Let them infuse for 1 to 2 hours, or overnight in the refrigerator.

Drain the cashews and place them in a blender. Strain the lilac flowers from the milk, reserving the milk and adding it to the blender with the butterfly pea flower powder, honey, salt, and melted coconut oil (if using). Discard the drained lilac flowers. Blend on high speed until completely creamy and smooth. Taste and add salt or more honey, if needed. Chill the mixture in the refrigerator until cold, and then pour the cream into an ice-cream maker and process until it is thickened and frozen. This will vary by ice-cream maker, but should take 10 to 15 minutes.

*continued »*

## NETTLE MOON COOKIES

2½ cups blanched almond flour or hazelnut flour

¼ cup tapioca flour

¾ teaspoon sea salt

¾ teaspoon baking soda

½ cup pure maple syrup

½ cup coconut oil, melted

2 teaspoons pure vanilla extract

2 to 4 dropperfuls of liquid chlorophyll (optional)

2 cups packed nettle leaves, well-blended in a food processor

3 to 6 tablespoons dried rose petals, plus more for sprinkling

Make the cookies: Mix together your almond flour, tapioca flour, salt, and baking soda in a large bowl. In a smaller bowl, whisk together the maple syrup, melted coconut oil, vanilla, and chlorophyll (if using). Place the nettles in a food processor or blender, and process well so they break up completely.

Stir the maple syrup mixture into the flour mixture, then fold in the processed nettles and rose petals. Once everything is mixed well, form a ball or tube of the dough, wrap it in parchment or wax paper, and chill it in the refrigerator for at least 2 hours.

Preheat the oven to 350°F and line two baking sheets with parchment paper. Remove the dough from the refrigerator. Use your hands to form about 2 tablespoons of dough at a time into a ball. Place the balls about 1 inch apart on the prepared baking sheets. They don't spread very much while baking, so they can be fairly close together. Flatten the dough balls to ¼- to ½-inch thickness with your palm. After they are flattened, use a circular cookie cutter or mason jar lid to make them into perfect disks.

Sprinkle more dried rose petals on top of each cookie and lightly press them into the dough. Bake for about 10 minutes, checking periodically to see whether they are becoming golden underneath. Remove from the oven when they are lightly golden, then let them cool completely on the pan. Once they are cool, place them in the freezer for 20 minutes to prepare them for receiving the ice cream.

To assemble, set out the lilac ice cream about 5 minutes before preparing the sandwiches. Use a butter knife to apply about 2 tablespoons per sandwich of the ice cream, to half of the cookies, turned bottom side up. Set another cookie, right side up, on the filling. If you want the sandwiches to look perfect, you can warm the knife in hot water and run it around the edges of the sandwiches to smooth out the ice cream. Once the sandwiches are made, put them back into the freezer to harden them again for at least an hour, then serve.

# WALK-IN-THE-GARDEN COOKIES

**MAKES 10 TO 12 COOKIES**

These are my favorite spring cookies with crisp edges and a slightly chewy center. They have a hint of caramelized flavor and are filled with spring violas. Violas are powerful little flowers, gentle in flavor and in their herbal medicinal properties; they're also soothing for stress, as well as being heart supportive. These cookies are a beautiful, easy way to bring the edible flowers of the season into your kitchen.

» **SIMPLE SWAPS** Substitute a gluten-free 1:1 flour blend for the oat flour and substitute any edible flowers for the violas. If you don't need these cookies to be dairy-free, the coconut oil can be replaced by soft unsalted butter.

1⅓ cups gluten-free oat flour

¼ teaspoon baking powder

½ teaspoon baking soda

¼ teaspoon salt

4 teaspoons chia or
   ground flaxseeds

¼ cup water

¼ cup plus 2 tablespoons solid but
   soft coconut oil

⅔ cup coconut sugar

1 teaspoon pure vanilla extract

¼ to ½ cup violas, violets,
   or pansies

**VARIATIONS** For a winter or fall cookie, these are delicious with ½ to 1 cup of chopped 63 to 72% chocolate of your choice, 1 tablespoon of finely powdered, sifted, roasted dandelion root, and a pinch of ground cinnamon.

Preheat the oven to 375°F and line a baking sheet with parchment paper. Whisk together the oat flour, baking powder, baking soda, and salt in a medium bowl. Prepare a flax egg by whisking together the ground chia or flax with the water in a small bowl. Set aside for 15 minutes to gel.

Combine the solid coconut oil and coconut sugar in a large bowl. Using a pastry cutter or fork, cut the sugar into the solid oil; this will take a few minutes. Cut until only small coconut oil clumps remain and the texture looks crumbly and wet. Add the flax egg and vanilla to the sugar mixture and stir until fully incorporated.

Using a hand mixer or a large spoon, gradually add the flour mixture to the sugar mixture. Mix until everything is well incorporated and a solid dough forms. Fold in the flowers.

Scoop balls of dough—about 2 tablespoons each—onto the prepared baking sheet, keeping the cookies well spaced apart. Bake for 9 to 12 minutes, until the cookies begin to get crisp on the edges. They will be extremely soft until they cool. Remove from the oven, transfer the cookies to a cooling rack, and let them cool completely before eating.

# VIOLET & WILD PLUM BLOSSOM FLAN

**SERVES 4**

This is a flan-inspired dessert without eggs or dairy, infused with the fragrant spell of wild plum blossoms and violets. Wild plum blossoms are transportive, and their medicine lies in their intoxicating floral and honey-almond scent. Violets are a sweet and delicious harbinger of spring, having been used medicinally to move lymph, and to detoxify and soothe the nervous system. This flan echoes the texture and flavor of the traditional egg flan and has a slightly salted caramel syrup. Flan originated in ancient Rome when there was a surplus of eggs, and original recipes were made with honey and sometimes eels or red pepper. Spanish culture embraced the custard and made it their own with the addition of the rich caramel sauce. This flan is a perfect treat for a spring day with the essence of the flowers in every bite.

✤ **FORAGER'S NOTE** Harvest plum blossoms and violets in the morning, when they are most fragrant and flavorful. Remove as many of the sticks or twigs as possible.

» **SIMPLE SWAP** Substitute 3 tablespoons of dried rose petals or 1½ tablespoons rose petal powder for the fresh blooms.

**CARAMEL SAUCE**
2 tablespoons coconut sugar
¼ cup water
1 tablespoon pure maple syrup
1 teaspoon pure vanilla extract
Pinch of sea salt

**FLAN**
1¼ cups full-fat coconut milk
(from one 13.5-ounce can)
½ cup wild plum blossoms or
violets, or a combination of the
two flowers
Scant 1 tablespoon
arrowroot powder
2 tablespoons honey
¼ teaspoon sea salt
½ teaspoon vanilla extract
½ teaspoon agar-agar powder (this
is different than agar flakes)

You can use ramekins or silicone molds for this recipe. I use shallow, 3-inch-wide "mini cake" silicone molds that I have on hand. If you use ramekins, you may need to slide a sharp knife around the rim to release the flan when serving, and the amount of flans that you have may be different depending on the size of your ramekins.

Prepare the caramel sauce: Combine all the sauce ingredients in a small skillet over medium heat and whisk them continuously until the sugar is dissolved and the mixture is bubbling. Turn off the heat and pour equal amounts of sauce into each ramekin or silicone mold, just enough to coat the bottom.

Make the flan: Heat the coconut milk in a medium saucepan over medium heat. Bring the milk to a boil, then immediately turn off the heat. Stir the plum blossoms into the milk. Cover and let the milk and flowers infuse for an hour in the refrigerator. Alternatively, prepare the night before and let them infuse overnight.

Strain the flowers through a mesh sieve over a bowl, to reserve the milk, pressing the flowers with the back of a spoon to squeeze them out completely. Discard the flowers. Transfer the coconut milk to a small saucepan and heat over low heat, then, leaving the rest in the pan, transfer a few tablespoons to a small cup or dish and stir the arrowroot powder into this portion of coconut milk so it becomes a slurry.

Add the honey, salt, and vanilla to the remaining coconut milk in the pan and continue to heat over low heat. Once the honey is dissolved, whisk the milk continuously as you add the agar-agar powder. Continue to whisk and heat for a minute or two, until the agar-agar powder dissolves and begins to thicken. While whisking quickly, add the arrowroot slurry and turn off the heat as soon as the mixture begins to thicken further; this will happen very fast.

Remove the thickened milk from the heat and pour the mixture equally into the prepared ramekins or molds—on top of the caramel sauce—then place them in the refrigerator. Allow the flan to totally solidify in the refrigerator for 3 to 5 hours.

When the flan has solidified, turn out the flans by placing a flat plate firmly on top of each ramekin or mold. Flip the two over so the flan and sauce come out together onto the plate or dish. If the flan is not releasing, run a knife around the edges and try flipping again. Eat right away or leave in the ramekins or molds, covered, in the refrigerator for up to 2 to 3 days before using.

# DANDELION SWITCHEL WITH MINT SUGAR RIM

### SERVES 2

Switchels are refreshing drinks, traditionally made with vinegar and honey or fruit, which likely originated in the Caribbean in the 1600s. They became popular in the 1800s in the United States for farm and field workers, and they also share similarities with oxymel, a honey-and-vinegar remedy dating back more than 2,000 years. In a way, switchels are the original energy drink, and provided much-needed electrolytes when people labored under hot and physically demanding conditions.

I have added dandelions to this version for an extra dose of nutrients, including potassium and vitamins A, C, and D and B vitamins. This recipe uses the whole dandelion plant, making it a perfect drink for attuning the body to spring and summer. For a fancier twist, add the mint sugar and lilac ice cubes, or serve the switchel on ice with a little muddled mint in the glass.

## LILAC ICE CUBES
¼ cup lilac blossoms, dandelions, or rose petals

Freshly squeezed lime juice, enough to fill an ice cube tray

## SWITCHEL
2 tablespoons Dandelion Vinegar (page 219)

2 tablespoons Dandelion Flower Syrup (page 218)

16 ounces sparkling water

## MINT RIM
3 tablespoons raw cane sugar or monk fruit granulated sweetener

3 tablespoons fresh mint leaves

½ teaspoon Dandelion Flower Syrup (page 218)

Make your ice cubes: Place your flowers in an empty ice cube tray, dividing them equally among the indentations. Pour the lime juice over the top of the flowers, then place the tray in the freezer to solidify.

Make the switchel: Combine the dandelion vinegar, dandelion flower syrup, and sparkling water in a mixing glass and stir.

Make the mint rim: Place the sugar and mint leaves in a coffee grinder or a spice grinder and process. Scoop the sugar mixture onto a small plate. On a separate plate, spread the dandelion flower syrup. Using your preferred switchel glass, dip the rim of the glass in the syrup and spin it so that the rim is entirely coated. Then, place the glass, rim side down, into the sugar mixture, coating the syrup in the mint sugar. If you have extra sugar, let it dry completely on a plate and then scoop into a jar to save for another time.

Flipping your glass right side up, pop in a few ice cubes and pour your switchel over the lilac ice.

# NETTLE "CHAMPAGNE"

**YIELD: APPROXIMATELY 1 GALLON**

I have been brewing herbal and medicinal fermented drinks and sodas, creating them at significant seasonal points in the year, marking the times of planting, harvest, and cycles of the natural world. Although this nettle brew is technically not Champagne, as it is not made in the Champagne region of France, it is made with Champagne yeast and is a dry, sparkling brew with all the healing benefits of nettles. Nettle "champagne" may be supportive for rheumatic and joint pains, seasonal allergies, and they can fortify and wake up the system in spring. This is not to say drinking alcohol is great for health, but it is merely another avenue of enjoying the medicinal properties of plants in moderation, with a little sparkle to accompany the medicine.

For this recipe, you will need a crock or large mason jar, or other nonreactive container to ferment your brew, and a cotton or muslin cloth to cover the container; plus, to bottle your brew, swing-top or plastic bottles with a secure screw-on top.

» **SIMPLE SWAP** If you do not have access to Champagne yeast, feel free to use an active dry yeast. You can also utilize wild yeasts from such plants as meadowsweet or elderflowers, with just a little sweetener and a few days' time. For this recipe, we are using a store-bought yeast to make a quick brew.

You can make this a nonalcoholic beverage by stopping the fermentation earlier in the process. It will be equally celebratory and delicious as a sparkling soda.

19 to 20 cups filtered, spring, or well water (see note)

2 pounds fresh nettles, or 2 to 3 cups dried

2 cups honey or sugar, plus 5 to 6 tablespoons to prime the bottles

2 to 3 tablespoons freshly squeezed lemon juice

1 heaping teaspoon cream of tartar

About 0.1 ounce Champagne yeast, or ¼ (2¼-teaspoon) packet active dry yeast

1 tablespoon lukewarm water (about 110°F)

Optional additions: 1 to 2 tablespoons fresh ginger, calendula, lemon balm, yarrow (bitter), dandelion (also bitter)

**NOTE** This is a very active home brew and can explode under pressure, so it is essential to use swing-top or screw-top bottles that lock tightly, and to open them cautiously. Additionally, chlorinated water can impede fermentation, so it's important to use water that isn't chlorinated, if possible.

Bring the water to a boil in a large pot, add the nettles, and simmer over medium-low heat for a few minutes. Turn off the heat and stir in the honey or sugar, lemon juice, and cream of tartar. Cover the pot with a tight lid and let steep for 4 to 6 hours, or overnight. After it has steeped, strain the liquid through a fine-mesh sieve into a crock, large mason jar, or nonreactive container. Squeeze the plants against the mesh with the back of a spoon to get as much of their juices in the pot as you can.

Mix your yeast with a tablespoon of lukewarm water in a small bowl. It is very important to activate the yeast this way first. Make sure your water is warm, not hot, or your yeast will die! Let the yeast sit for 20 minutes before adding to your completely cool brew. Cover the brew with a clean cotton towel or cloth and secure it across the opening. Let sit on the counter for 3 to 4 days.

If you are making a nonalcoholic soda, let sit for only 24 hours. This will stop the fermentation process, but it will still be bubbly.

Ready a set of swing-top or screw-top bottles. Strain the liquid again through cheesecloth or mesh into a large measuring cup or something that makes it easier to pour into the bottles. Stir 5 to 6 tablespoons of honey or sugar into the brew to get it really active again before bottling. The sweetener will be eaten up by the yeast, which will create more fermentation, resulting in bubbles/carbonation.

Pour into your bottles and seal. Label the bottles with the date, contents, and herbal love notes. Let the sealed bottles sit out for 8 to 24 hours, or place them directly in the refrigerator. These bottles must be opened with care over a sink, as they are known to have built up pressure and can be explosive. Tilt away from your face while opening.

# SUMMER

# CUCUMBER, CUCAMELON & PURSLANE SALAD WITH WILDFLOWERS

### SERVES 2 TO 4

This is a cooling, crisp salad with the crunch and citrus flavors of purslane, cucumber, and currants, and the balance of vinegar, flower salts, and garlic. Cucamelon is a Mexican sour gherkin. Purslane is an amazing edible and medicinal "weed." It has the highest omega-3 fatty acid content of any vegetable, is packed with vitamins A, C, E, and K, and contains loads of minerals. Luckily for us, it grows prolifically across the world, from abandoned lots to your own backyard, forests, and along seashores.

❊ **FORAGER'S NOTE** Purslane has a poisonous lookalike called spurge that has a milky white latex when cut. Purslane does not ooze a milky white substance; always double-check in a foraging book when harvesting any wild plants.

» **SIMPLE SWAP** Leave out the currants or purslane if you can't find them, adding extra cucumber in their place.

1 to 2 large garlic cloves, chopped finely

2 to 3 tablespoons ume plum vinegar or cider vinegar

1½ to 2 cups cucumbers, lightly crushed and chopped

½ cup or handful of purslane leaves

½ cup or handful of cucamelons or more cucumbers

2 tablespoons borage flowers or other edible flowers such as blue cornflower petals

1 tablespoon fresh currants (optional)

Salt

Edible fresh flowers, for garnish

Stir together the garlic and vinegar in a small bowl and let sit as you prepare the rest of the salad. Combine the remaining ingredients, including salt to taste, in a large bowl and pour the garlic mixture over the top. Mix everything together and cover, then chill in the refrigerator for 20 minutes to overnight before serving. Before serving, add the fresh edible flowers to the top. This can be eaten right away, but the garlic will mellow over time in the refrigerator.

# SOBA NOODLE SALAD WITH SESAME NETTLES

**SERVES 4**

Buckwheat soba noodle salad is a refreshing, light meal for a warm spring or summer day. Buckwheat is a gluten-free pseudocereal that is known for its cooling and soothing properties, and it may support blood sugar balance and heart health. Nettles are a nutrient-dense herb, providing vitamins and minerals, protein, and mood-boosting and healing properties. I like to make a spring "nest" of the soba noodles and add the sesame nettles to the center with a slightly spicy radish, spring carrots, and golden shiitake mushrooms. Soba can be dressed up with any fresh vegetables and herbs you have on hand.

» **SIMPLE SWAP** Use spinach or kale in place of nettles.

**SALAD**

One 8- to 10-ounce package dried soba noodles, prepared and then rinsed under cold water for 3 minutes

1½ tablespoons soy sauce

1½ tablespoons sesame oil

1 tablespoon toasted sesame oil

3 tablespoons brown or white rice vinegar

2 teaspoons minced fresh ginger

1 to 2 teaspoons mirin

2 teaspoons pure maple syrup

2 teaspoons sesame or olive oil for cooking

2 garlic cloves, chopped

1½ to 2 cups shiitake mushrooms (fresh or dried and rehydrated), chopped

Sea salt

2 to 3 carrots, shredded finely

½ daikon radish, sliced in very thin rounds

2 tablespoons sesame seeds for serving

Make the salad: Prepare the soba noodles according to the package directions and be careful not to overcook; al dente is best, so they don't get too soft in the salad. Set aside.

For the sauce, whisk together the soy sauce, sesame oil, toasted sesame oil, rice vinegar, ginger, mirin, and maple syrup in a medium bowl. Set aside.

Heat the sesame oil in a medium skillet over medium heat. Add the garlic, and stir until golden. Then, add the mushrooms. Let the mushrooms release their juices and suck them back up, sprinkle with salt, and continue to cook until the mushrooms get crispy and golden on the edges, 5 to 7 minutes. Once they are crispy, remove the mushrooms from the heat and add to the sauce and stir. Allow the mushrooms to marinate while you prepare the nettles.

Make the sesame nettles: Bring a large pot of water to a boil. Blanch the nettles in the boiling water for 1 to 3 minutes, just until softened. Then, drain the nettles and immediately run them under very cold water until they're completely cooled. Squeeze any remaining water from the nettles and fluff them in a little bowl.

## SESAME NETTLES

4 cups fresh nettles, steamed or blanched, then cooled under cold running water

1 tablespoon sesame seeds—half black, half white

1 teaspoon soy sauce

1 tablespoon sesame oil

1 teaspoon sliced spring onion, chopped finely in rings

1 garlic clove, minced

¼ teaspoon sea salt

Dry toast the mixed sesame seeds in a small, dry skillet over medium heat, stirring constantly, until fragrant and golden. Scoop the seeds into a mortar and pestle and grind most of them, leaving some of them whole. Transfer the ground sesame seeds to a small bowl and whisk in the soy sauce, sesame oil, spring onion, garlic, and salt. Pour the mixture over the nettles and stir to incorporate.

Assemble the salad: Mix together the carrots, radish, noodles, mushrooms, and the sauce in a large serving bowl. You can leave this mixture in the bowl or transfer to a large plate, form a nest, and add the sesame nettles to the center, or simply top the noodle salad with the nettles. Sprinkle with additional sesame seeds to serve.

# CARROT & TOMATO SOUP WITH CUCUMBER & SWEET CORN QUICK PICKLE

**SERVES 4 TO 6**

This soup is a piquant taste of summer with fresh tomato, carrots, and sweet corn pickle. It comes together quickly and can be served with a fresh salad for an easy summer meal. Many years ago, when I was on a trip in Ireland, I was caught in a deluge of November rain with one of my best friends, Holly, in a little coffee shop. We split a bowl of what was simply labeled "vegetable soup," and surprisingly, it was one of the best soups I have ever tasted. This variation was inspired by that soup and Indian cuisine, boosted by the addition of fried spices, all topped with a fresh summer veggie quick "pickle."

» **SIMPLE SWAPS** If you don't have marigold leaf for the quick pickle, use cilantro, parsley, or another fresh herb of your choice. Scarlet begonias have a citrus flavor, and can be replaced with any flower you like, or leave them out. Lemon or lime juice works here; both are delicious and work great either way.

1½ cups chopped cucumbers or cucamelons, or a combination, cut in small, rough chunks

1 ear fresh sweet corn

Juice of 1 to 2 lemons or limes (3 to 4 tablespoons juice)

½ teaspoon sea salt, plus more to taste

For garnish: ⅛ to ¼ cup scarlet begonias and/or marigold leaf

**SOUP**

2 tablespoons olive oil

2 garlic cloves, chopped

1 medium yellow onion, chopped roughly

5 cups summer squash

6 to 10 medium carrots, chopped roughly

2 cups roughly chopped fresh or canned tomatoes

6 to 8 cups vegetable broth or water

1 tablespoon turmeric powder

Sea salt

1 to 2 tablespoons coconut oil or ghee

2 tablespoons black or brown mustard seeds

1 tablespoon cumin seeds

2 teaspoons fennel seeds

⅛ teaspoon asafetida (hing) powder (optional)

Prepare the quick pickle: Combine the cucumbers and corn in a medium bowl, then mix the lemon juice and salt into the vegetables. Do not add the garnish at this time. Cover and chill in the refrigerator for at least an hour while you make the soup.

Make the soup: Heat the oil in a large, heavy-bottomed soup pot over medium heat. Add the garlic and sauté for a minute or so, stirring until it becomes golden and releases its scent, then stir in the onion, cooking until it becomes translucent. Add the summer squash and let cook until slightly soft, about 3 minutes. Add the carrots and tomatoes, and stir to combine everything.

Pour the broth or water over the vegetables and bring to a boil. Lower the heat to low and simmer until the carrots are soft enough to blend, about 10 minutes. The flavor of the carrot should still be strong, so make sure to cook until just soft.

Working in batches, transfer the soup to a large blender and blend until smooth, returning to the pot when you've finished blending. Alternatively, you can use a hand blender to blend the soup inside the pot. Stir the turmeric into the soup.

Heat the coconut oil in a small skillet over medium heat. When the oil is hot, add the mustard seeds, and once they begin popping, quickly add the cumin and fennel seeds, stirring so that nothing burns. Add the asafetida once the seeds begin to release their scent. Stir, turn off the heat, then pour the mixture into the soup. It will sizzle and pop, so be careful not to burn yourself. Mix in the spices well and ladle into bowls.

Remove your quick pickle from the fridge and garnish with the begonias and/or marigold leaf. Generously spoon the pickle onto the soup, or eat as a side salad.

# RAINBOW PUPUSAS WITH FORAGED FILLINGS & SALSA RIOJA

**SERVES 4**

Pupusas originated in El Salvador and are made with masa corn flour that has been nix-tamalized. They are traditionally filled with chicharrón (cracklings), cheese, beans, or vegetables, and these contain a combination of foraged plants, mushrooms, and beans. I have always loved pupusas and began making them in summer with greens I was gathering and, for the salsa rioja, fresh tomatoes we grew ourselves. I encourage you to use what you have on hand seasonally. Traditionally, these are served with curtido (cabbage relish) and salsa rioja, which makes a complete summer meal.

» **SIMPLE SWAPS**  Any filling you want can replace what is suggested here. Omit the colorings and just use the masa as it is.

## FILLING
½ cup pinto beans, cooked and drained, or canned, drained and rinsed

1 tablespoon olive oil

3 garlic cloves, chopped finely

2 cups assorted greens, roughly chopped (dandelion, nettles, violet leaf, chard, kale, etc.)

1 to 2 teaspoons sea salt

½ cup shredded vegan or dairy white Cheddar cheese or queso blanco of your choice

3 green onions, chopped

## PUPUSAS
3 cups masa corn flour (this is different from cornstarch or cornmeal—it must say "masa" or "masa harina" on the package and must have been nixtamalized)

2 teaspoons sea salt

2½ to 2¾ cups water

About 3 tablespoons oil, plus more for your hands

Begin the filling: Place the pinto beans in a small bowl and mash lightly with a fork. Heat the oil in a medium skillet over medium heat, then add the garlic and sauté until fragrant. Add the greens and stir until they are just cooked and wilted. Add salt to taste, remove from the heat, and set aside.

Make the pupusas: Whisk the masa corn flour and salt together in a large bowl. Slowly mix in the water, starting with a smaller amount of water and adding more, if needed, to bring the dough together. It should be soft and moldable in your hand. Divide the dough into four equal pieces and place them in separate small bowls to make the colorful pupusas; if you aren't adding color, just skip the next step.

Add your preferred colorful powders (see variations below) to the dough portions. If you are making your pupusas green, place your fresh nettles in a food processor and blend well. Then, add one of the dough balls and blend again, pulsing to incorporate the nettles. Remove the dough from the food processor and reform the dough with your hands.

*continued »*

To create pupusas of
different colors, add
these ingredients to your
masa mixture:

GREEN  ½ cup fresh nettles;
1 to 2 dropperfuls of liquid chlorophyll per
ball of dough

BLUE  1 tablespoon butterfly pea flower
powder per ball of dough

PURPLE  1 tablespoon purple sweet potato
powder per ball of dough

YELLOW  1 to 2 teaspoons turmeric powder
per ball of dough

**FOR SERVING**
Purple Curtido-Cabbage Quick
    Pickle (page 222)
1 recipe Salsa Rioja
    (recipe follows)

Assemble and cook the pupusas: Fill a small bowl with water, pouring a small amount of oil on top. Dip your fingers in this bowl between forming the pupusas to keep the dough from sticking to your hands.

Heat a large skillet over medium heat and add about 3 tablespoons of olive oil to the pan. Scoop 3 tablespoons of dough into your hand and roll it into a ball. Now, on a clean surface, smash the dough into a flat pancake with your hands, dipping your hands into the water bowl as needed.

In the center of the pupusa, add a few teaspoons of mashed pinto beans, greens, cheese, and/or green onions in any combination, and close the dough like a satchel, carefully folding and sealing it around the filling. The pupusa will crack and separate, but this is okay! Just keep flattening, and fold and spread the dough over the openings. Form the dough into a disk about 1 inch thick and 3 to 4 inches in diameter.

Place the sealed and flattened pupusa in the heated oil, and cook on both sides until crisp and golden, 3 to 5 minutes per side. Continue in this way until all are prepared and cooked. Serve immediately with Salsa Rioja, quick pickle, and/or a tomato salsa.

## SALSA RIOJA

**MAKES 2 CUPS**

2 cups tomatoes peeled, seeded,
    and chopped
¼ cup chopped onion
1 garlic clove, chopped
3 tablespoons olive oil
2 tablespoons fresh wild or
    regular oregano, chopped, or
    2 teaspoons dried
Sea salt and freshly ground
    black pepper
Sprinkle of cayenne pepper

Preheat the oven to 400°F. Arrange the tomatoes, onion, and garlic in a single layer on a baking sheet and coat with the olive oil. Roast for 10 to 15 minutes, or until the tomatoes "melt" and the onion softens. Scoop the roasted vegetables into a blender and add the oregano, salt, black pepper to taste, and a sprinkle of cayenne for a little heat. Blend on high speed, then pour into a bowl to serve with the pupusas or Mini Rainbow Socca (page 57).

# SEASONAL PETAL ROLLS WITH TAMARIND & PEANUT SAUCE

**SERVES 4 TO 6**

Petal rolls, or spring rolls, are a beautiful way to eat all the fresh veggies, flowers, and fruits of the season. Spring rolls have a long history that likely originates in China with fried spring rolls, but they are popular in Vietnam, where it is an iconic dish called gỏi cuốn in the south, nem cuốn in the north, and bánh cuốn in central Vietnam, names that mean, respectively, summer, spring, or fresh rolls. Think of the rolls as little paintings: adding flowers first and then building a "background" of dark leafy greens, then noodles and other veggies, layering different colors and textures throughout.

» **SIMPLE SWAP** All the ingredients listed are meant to inspire, but use what you have available or what is in season. I follow a general framework of one-third crunchy ingredients, such as cucumber or carrot; one-third softer vegetables or fruits, such as avocado or peach; and one-third flowers and herbs, such as mint, cilantro, and violas.

*continued »*

One 8-ounce package spring roll rice wrappers

½ cup edible flowers, stemmed (scarlet begonias, nasturtiums, rose petals, etc.)

½ to 1 cup leaves of your choice (spinach, lettuce, nasturtium leaves, marigold, etc.), torn

2 small cucumbers or zucchini, cut in thin, lengthwise strips

1 to 2 cups crisp vegetables (asparagus, bell pepper, sugar peas, green apple, etc.) in an assortment of colors, sliced lengthwise in thin, roughly 2- to 3-inch-long strips

½ cup softer vegetables or fruits (avocado, mango, peach), sliced in thin, lengthwise strips

2 cups fresh mint, cilantro, basil, and/or shiso, chopped roughly

One 10-ounce package very thin rice noodles, prepared according to the package instructions and cooled

½ cup protein of your choice, such as tofu

1 recipe Tamarind & Peanut Sauce (recipe follows)

Ready all your ingredients on your counter or table so you can see your "palette." Fill a bowl with water that is wide enough to dip the spring roll wrappers into it. Next to this, set a large, flat plate that will be your workspace. Quickly dip a rice wrapper into the water and place it on the plate. As you work, remember to leave about ½ inch uncovered margin around the perimeter of the wrapper so that you can seal the roll at the end.

Starting in the center of the wrapper, add four or five whole flowers or large flower petals. Add the background leaves, such as lettuce, on top of the flowers, in a single layer. Then, make a line of cucumber strips and your crisp vegetables. Use up to seven strips in this center line; they can be close together and on top of one another. Then, layer on your softer vegetables or fruits next to or on top of the crisp vegetables, still maintaining a line. Sprinkle with your preferred herbs, 2 to 5 tablespoons total per roll, depending on your tastes. Add a small amount of noodles, any protein, and any other ingredient you would like to include on top of this center line.

To roll, rotate the wrap so that the line of fillings is parallel to the edge of your counter or table. Then, slowly lift one side of the wrap using both hands, folding it away from yourself and over the line of fillings. Tuck the folded side of the wrap under the fillings, and fold the left and right sides of the wrap inward as well. Now, carefully continue rolling up the wrap into a tight burrito shape. Sometimes I leave the sides open to show the inside of the roll, but this is optional. Repeat this assembly-and-rolling process until all your wraps are used.

Serve your rolls alongside Tamarind & Peanut Sauce for dipping.

# TAMARIND & PEANUT SAUCE

**MAKES 4 TO 6 SERVINGS**

½ cup crunchy peanut butter without added oils, sugar, or additives

1 cup full-fat coconut milk, plus more to taste or thin

2 tablespoons pure maple syrup or sweetener of your choice

1 heaping tablespoon tamarind paste

1 tablespoon freshly squeezed lime juice

1½ tablespoons soy sauce

2 teaspoons grated fresh ginger

¼ teaspoon sea salt, or to taste

Sprinkle of cayenne pepper

Combine all the ingredients in a medium saucepan and heat over low heat, whisking until well blended. If you like a thicker consistency, leave the sauce as is and know that it will thicken when it cools. If you like a thinner sauce, you can add water or coconut milk, 1 tablespoon at a time, while heating over low heat, until the sauce reaches your desired consistency.

When the sauce ingredients have fully incorporated, taste and adjust the seasonings accordingly, adding more salt as necessary. Remove the sauce from the heat and allow to cool. Serve alongside the seasonal petal rolls.

# HOLLYHOCK WRAPS (DOLMAS) WITH ROSE TAHINI SAUCE

**SERVES 4 AS A SALAD COURSE**

Traditionally, dolmas and sarmas are made with grape leaves and stuffed with slow-cooked rice or vegetables. One day, while dreaming of dolmas, I noticed my hollyhocks had large leaves that might work in place of grape leaves. Hollyhocks have long been a culinary muse, from their palm-size edible leaves to their lightly flavored and brilliantly colored flowers. I like to limit stove and oven use in the hotter months, making this dish an even more perfect summer recipe, as it requires very little actual cooking aside from a briny dip in salted water and rice or grain preparation.

To add an additional flavor element, the rose tahini sauce is the ultimate pairing. This sauce has the cooling and astringent benefits of rose and can be added to dressings, soups, and other sauces.

» **SIMPLE SWAPS**  Use brined grape leaves if you do not have access to hollyhocks, and use quinoa or any grain of your choice in place of rice. You can use any mushroom in place of lion's mane, or leave it out if you prefer.

12 to 18 large hollyhock leaves

2 tablespoons olive oil

1 garlic clove, crushed
     and chopped

1½ cups lion's mane mushrooms,
     chopped finely

¾ teaspoon baharat seasoning

¾ teaspoon sea salt

½ cup edible fresh flowers (rose
     petals, chive flowers, calendula,
     etc.) or mild-flavored greens,
     such as salad mix or lettuces

1 cup cooked rice or quinoa

2 teaspoons freshly squeezed
     lemon juice

2 tablespoons drained tomatoes

1 teaspoon fresh cilantro,
     chopped finely

1 tablespoon finely
     chopped scallions

1 recipe Rose Tahini Sauce
     (recipe follows)

Add ice to a bowl of water that is large enough to fit all the hollyhock leaves, and set aside. Combine ¼ to ½ cup of sea salt and 4 cups of water in a large pot on the stove and bring to a boil. Add the hollyhock leaves and blanch them for 2 minutes. Immediately drain and plunge them into the ice bath for a minute to stop the cooking and keep them bright green.

Heat the olive oil in a medium skillet and add the garlic, cooking for just 2 minutes. Add the mushrooms and continue to fry, stirring regularly. Add ½ teaspoon of the baharat seasoning and ¼ teaspoon of the salt. Continue to stir until the mushrooms release their moisture and absorb it again, getting slightly crisp and golden.

Finely chop the edible flowers or greens and set them aside. Place the rice in a medium bowl. Stir in the mushrooms, lemon juice, tomatoes, remaining ½ teaspoon of salt, and remaining ¼ teaspoon of baharat seasoning. Fold the flowers or greens, cilantro, and scallions into the rice mixture and mix until well incorporated.

Ready a plate to the side. Take a hollyhock leaf from the ice bath and fold it in half lengthwise. Cut a very small semicircle, just a small amount, off the bottom of the leaf. Open the leaf, vein side up, and place 1 to 2 teaspoons of the filling in the center of the leaf, just above where you cut the stem. Leave a large amount of leaf around the filling so it is easy to roll. Bring the bottom of the leaf, near the stem cut, up over the mixture. Tuck in the sides of the leaf and roll forward toward the top of the leaf. Keep tucking the side parts as you roll until the leaf is rolled all the way. Place, seam side down, on the plate. Repeat this process until you run out of filling.

Serve with Rose Tahini Sauce or eat on its own.

*continued* »

# ROSE TAHINI SAUCE

**MAKES 4 SERVINGS**

2 tablespoons tahini

1 tablespoon olive oil, plus
more to finish

2 teaspoons water, plus
more as needed

1 teaspoon sea salt

1 teaspoon rose powder

½ teaspoon freshly squeezed
lemon juice

Sprinkle of baharat or
harissa seasoning

1 teaspoon purple carrot powder
(optional, for color)

Paprika to finish

Combine the tahini, olive oil, water, salt, rose powder, lemon juice, baharat, and purple carrot powder (if using) in a small bowl and mix with a fork until everything is incorporated. Depending on the consistency of your tahini, you may need to add more water; do so a little at a time until to your liking. Add more salt and lemon to taste. Finish with a drizzle of olive oil and a dusting of paprika. Serve with the hollyhock wraps.

**NOTE**  Pure rose petals are the best thing to use for this recipe, as rosewater or rose flavoring will overpower the sauce.

# GARDEN-INSPIRED PAD THAI

**SERVES 4**

The first time I traveled beyond the United States, I went to Thailand for a month, immersing myself in the culture of food there; it is the only place I ever took a cooking course, and it changed the way I viewed food and the balance of flavor. I spent afternoons and nights wandering the prolific markets, eating everything along the way. Pad thai carts at midnight in Bangkok were some of my favorite stops; they offered a deceptively simple noodle dish, but one that offers endless possibilities in flavor. Every cart had hot chiles in vinegar, which is now a staple item in my kitchen that goes on noodles and soups. Thai peppers are traditional, but serranos and other hot peppers will work great here. This dish can be adjusted according to season, and any protein you like can be added in place of mushrooms. I like to have a huge array of raw vegetables in summer that can be mixed into the noodles or placed around the serving dish.

» **SIMPLE SWAPS** Instead of mushrooms, substitute 1 cup of chopped tofu or other protein of your choice. Omit the eggs if you do not eat them. Use the seasonal vegetables of your choice. Thai bird's-eye peppers are traditional, but serranos and other spicy peppers will work in their place.

*continued* »

¼ cup rice vinegar

1 to 2 medium hot red peppers,
    chopped in thin rounds

**PAD THAI**

10 ounces uncooked pad thai
    rice noodles

3 to 4 tablespoons sesame or
    coconut oil

1 to 1½ cups lion's mane, oyster, or
    cremini mushrooms, chopped

2 garlic cloves, smashed
    and chopped

3 tablespoons fish sauce or vegan
    fish sauce

2 tablespoons tamarind paste

3 tablespoons soy sauce

3 tablespoons coconut sugar or
    granulated sugar

2 large eggs, beaten

1 to 2 cups vegetable
    broth or water

½ cup sliced green onion (cut
    diagonally in 2-inch pieces)

2 cups assorted raw or blanched
    vegetables (broccoli, snap
    peas, summer squash, carrots,
    etc.), chopped or sliced thinly

½ cup fresh basil

¼ cup fresh cilantro leaves,
    chopped, or a sprinkle of green
    coriander berries

3 tablespoons toasted
    peanuts, chopped

2 limes, quartered

Prepare the chiles in vinegar (if using) at least 24 hours in advance: Pour the vinegar into a small glass jar, add the sliced pepper, and let marinate for at least 24 hours. Keep in the pantry in a cool, dark place.

Make the pad thai: Place the noodles in a large bowl and add enough water to cover them, allowing them to soak as you cook the mushrooms. Place a bowl next to the stove to receive the cooked mushrooms. Pour enough sesame oil into a large skillet or wok to coat the bottom (you shouldn't be using all the oil), heat over medium-high heat, and sauté the mushrooms, about 7 minutes. Once the mushrooms begin to release liquid and brown, add the garlic and more oil, if necessary. Cook only for 2 minutes or so longer, then transfer the mushrooms to the waiting bowl.

Place a scant 3 tablespoons of the fish sauce, reserving ¼ teaspoon of it, in a small bowl, and stir in the tamarind paste, soy sauce, and coconut sugar. In a separate small bowl, whisk together the beaten eggs, reserved ¼ teaspoon of fish sauce, and ¼ teaspoon of the sesame oil.

Return the large skillet to the stove over medium heat and add enough oil to coat the bottom. Add the noodles and ½ cup of the broth or water, plus all the tamarind mixture, and stir to incorporate. Turn the heat way down, add 1½ cups more broth, and cover with a heavy lid. Stir frequently while the noodles cook so they don't stick together or to the pan. The noodles should cook for 7 to 10 minutes.

Once the noodles are al dente, transfer them on the serving plate and add a small amount of oil to the skillet, coating the bottom. Add the beaten egg mixture and, moving quickly, lightly scramble the eggs. Add the noodles and mushrooms back to the pan, along with the green onion. Stir everything to incorporate. Taste and add soy sauce, if needed. Serve with all the vegetables, basil, and cilantro, adding peanuts to the top, offering more on the side. Fresh lime quarters and the chiles in vinegar are the perfect final touch.

# NETTLE DOUGHNUTS WITH BUTTERFLY PEA FLOWER ICING & MARIGOLDS

**MAKES 9 DOUGHNUTS**

These doughnuts were inspired by two beloved plants, nettles and oats. The combination of nettles with an electric blue icing and glowing orange marigolds is one of my favorite colorful desserts. Cake doughnuts are a nostalgic treat; my beloved grandfather and I ate them on our "coffee break" after chores in the summers I spent with my grandparents in rural Massachusetts. Today, I see doughnuts as one of the ways to create a bridge between plants and people, sharing something like a stinging nettle in a fun, recognizable treat. Doughnuts have become a medium to convey the color, scent, and flavor of a plant.

» **SIMPLE SWAP** If you can't get fresh nettles, add 3 tablespoons of powdered dried nettles to your dry ingredients while making the doughnuts.

## DOUGHNUTS

Oil for pan

1 cup loosely packed fresh nettle leaf

1½ cups blanched almond flour

1 cup oat flour

¼ cup coconut flour

½ teaspoon baking soda

½ teaspoon salt

4 large eggs, whisked

½ cup pure maple syrup

½ cup coconut milk

1 tablespoon pure vanilla extract

½ cup melted coconut oil

Make the doughnuts: Preheat the oven to 350°F and lightly oil a nine-well doughnut mold. Remove the leaves from the nettles, using gloves, and blanch the nettles in a medium saucepan of boiling water, about 1 minute. Drain the nettles and immediately place them in very cold or ice water to stop them from cooking. Drain and lightly squeeze out the nettles to remove the ice water. Then, process them well in a food processor and set aside.

Whisk together the almond flour, oat flour, coconut flour, baking soda, and salt in a large bowl, breaking up any clumps. Whisk together the eggs, maple syrup, coconut milk, and vanilla in a medium bowl. Fold the egg mixture into the flour mixture. Then, add the melted coconut oil in a slow stream, whisking the whole time. Fold in the nettles, mixing well.

Spoon the batter evenly into the prepared doughnut wells and bake for 25 to 30 minutes, until a toothpick inserted into a doughnut comes out clean. Remove the doughnuts from the mold by flipping them onto a cooling rack. Allow them to cool before applying the frosting.

*continued »*

## ICING

8 ounces maple butter

2 tablespoons butterfly pea
flower powder

½ teaspoon coconut
cream (optional)

1 teaspoon blue
spirulina (optional)

Sprinkle of marigold petals, green
bottoms removed

Sprinkle of nettle seeds

Make the frosting: Place the maple butter in a small bowl and whisk in the butterfly pea flower powder. Spread this frosting evenly over each doughnut. If you want to make two different colored frostings, before spreading, you can spoon about half of the maple butter into another small bowl and add about ½ teaspoon coconut cream and the blue spirulina. Mix well and drizzle this lighter color on top of the darker frosting for variation.

Sprinkle with marigold petals and nettle seeds, or other edible flowers, to decorate.

# CHOKECHERRY SORBET

**SERVES 4 TO 6**

On the last hot days of summer, we collect baskets of chokecherries as the sun sets, to make sorbet and syrups. Chokecherries are a tart little stone fruit that has been a staple medicinal food for Indigenous peoples for thousands of years. They are prolific, identified as an invasive plant in many places, and are rich in anthocyanin and vitamin C.

As do all stone fruits, chokecherry pits contain a compound that turns into cyanide in the digestive system if cracked open. It would likely take a large amount of cracked stone fruit pits to cause any kind of poisoning, but always heat them for at least 15 to 20 minutes, to be safe.

» **SIMPLE SWAP** If you don't have chokecherries, feel free to substitute another fruit in its place, tasting and adjusting for sweetness.

---

4 cups chokecherries

4 cups water

½ cup honey or sweetener of your choice

1 to 2 tablespoons freshly squeezed lemon juice


**VARIATION** Add a generous tablespoon of Hawthorn Berry Brandy (page 171) or any brandy you'd like, for a slightly boozy and bright sorbet

Combine the chokecherries and water in a large saucepan over medium-high heat, cover, and simmer for 15 to 20 minutes. Turn off the heat and stir in the honey and lemon juice until the honey dissolves. Strain through a mesh sieve, squeezing the chokecherries hard with a heavy spoon, and composting or discarding the chokecherries.

Cool the liquid completely in the refrigerator before transferring to an ice-cream maker and churning per your machine's instructions. If you don't have an ice-cream maker, freeze the mixture, then whisk or blend it every 20 minutes until it reaches a thick, frozen consistency. Spoon the sorbet into bowls to serve.

# MEADOWSWEET & FIREWEED MADEIRA CAKE

**MAKES 8 TO 10 SERVINGS**

I was inspired to create this version of the cake with meadowsweet flowers and Fermented Fireweed Tea/Ivan Chai (page 124). Despite its Portuguese name, Madeira cake is actually a British pound cake made with almond and lemon that was traditionally served with Madeira wine, but is nowadays served with a strong tea. Meadowsweet is an intensely fragrant flower with heady notes of floral almond, often referred to as "nature's aspirin" because of its purported pain-relieving capabilities. It pairs perfectly with the deep flavors of Ivan Chai and makes a cake that smells beautifully of summer.

» **SIMPLE SWAP** If you cannot find meadowsweet or fireweed tea, grate the zest of an entire lemon into your batter, add ⅛ to ¼ teaspoon almond extract, and infuse rose petals or other fragrant edible flowers. Alternatively, you can add the zest and almond extract, and leave out the flowers, but I prefer the floral scent of this cake!

One 13.5-ounce can full-fat coconut milk

½ cup fresh meadowsweet flowers, or ¼ cup dried

2 tablespoons Fermented Fireweed Tea/Ivan Chai (page 124)

Oil for pan

2 cups very fine white rice flour, plus more for dusting

2 tablespoons baking powder

¼ teaspoon salt

4 large eggs, at room temperature

1¼ cups coconut sugar

2 tablespoons butter of your choice, melted

1 teaspoon pure vanilla extract

Zest of 1 lemon

Jam and cream of your choice for serving (optional)

Heat the coconut milk in a small saucepan over medium heat until just simmering. Turn off the heat and add the flowers and fireweed tea, covering with a tight lid. Let infuse for 4 hours or in the fridge overnight, then strain through a fine-mesh sieve in the morning, reserving the milk. You may need to warm it again slightly to strain it, as the coconut milk may solidify slightly. As you strain, squeeze the flowers by pressing them against the mesh sieve with a spoon, then discard them.

Preheat the oven to 350°F. Oil and flour a 9-by-5-inch loaf pan. Whisk together the rice flour, baking powder, and salt in a large bowl. In a medium bowl, whisk together the eggs, then add the sugar, melted butter, strained infused coconut milk, vanilla, and lemon zest. Add the egg mixture to the flour mixture and mix well. Pour the batter into your prepared loaf pan and bake for 20 to 25 minutes, checking for doneness by inserting a toothpick into the center and making sure it comes out clean.

**ICING/GLAZE**

¼ cup honey or icing sugar

Zest of 1 lemon

2 tablespoons freshly squeezed
lemon juice

2 tablespoons elderflower cordial

While the cake bakes, make the glaze: Whisk together honey, lemon zest and juice, and elderflower cordial in a small bowl. When the cake has baked through, remove it from the oven and pour the glaze over it while the cake is still warm.

Serve the cake with jam and cream, or leave it plain, and enjoy with a cup of Fermented Fireweed Tea, black tea, or Madeira wine.

# LEMON BALM & LIME CURD THUMBPRINT COOKIES

**MAKES 1 DOZEN COOKIES**

These cookies are lightly sweet and chewy with a tangy lime and lemon balm curd center. Lemon balm, a vibrant mint family plant, has been used for soothing the nervous system and the heart. As soon as the soft green leaves unfurl in summer, I find myself drawn in, stirring them into sweet and savory dishes alike; this bright and silky curd is always at the top of my list.

» **SIMPLE SWAP** Replace the fresh leaves with 2 tablespoons very well-powdered, dried lemon balm, whisked in with your dry ingredients.

2½ cups blanched almond flour or hazelnut flour

¼ cup tapioca flour

¾ teaspoon sea salt

¾ teaspoon baking soda

2 cups lemon balm leaves, stemmed

½ cup coconut, melted, or neutral oil

2 teaspoons pure vanilla extract

½ cup pure maple syrup

4 to 5 dropperfuls of liquid chlorophyll or green food dye (optional)

Whisk together the almond flour, tapioca flour, salt, and baking soda in a large bowl. Mix together the melted coconut oil, vanilla, maple syrup, and chlorophyll (if using) in a small bowl.

Process the lemon balm very well in a food processor or blender. Scrape the lemon balm paste out of the device and set aside. Stir the oil mixture into the flour mixture, and then fold in the lemon balm paste. In the end, you should have a moldable dough. Form a ball or tube of the dough, wrap it in parchment paper or beeswax wrap, and place in the refrigerator for at least 2 hours.

Preheat your oven to 350°F. Line two baking sheets with parchment. Remove the dough from the refrigerator. Cut or break off about 2 tablespoons of dough and shape it into a ball, pressing a thumbprint in the center and setting the dough ball, indentation up, on a prepared baking sheet. (The indentations will pop up again while baking.) Repeat this process until all your dough is shaped and placed 1 inch apart on the pans. Bake for 10 to 14 minutes, checking to see whether they are browning. They should become golden underneath and lightly on the top.

When the cookies are done, pull them out, and while they are warm, gently press down again in the center of each cookie to reestablish their thumbprint. Let cool completely while you prepare the lime and lemon balm curd.

### CURD

½ cup full-fat coconut milk

¼ cup freshly squeezed lime juice

1 cup lemon balm leaves

2 teaspoons lime zest

½ cup honey

1 to 2 dropperfuls concentrated chlorophyll or green food dye (optional)

1½ tablespoons cornstarch, tapioca starch, or arrowroot powder

Make the curd: Combine the coconut milk and lime juice in a small saucepan and bring to a simmer over medium heat. Add the lemon balm leaves, heating them until they "melt" into the liquid. Cover with a lid and turn off the heat. Let the leaves steep for 10 minutes.

After 10 minutes, strain the mixture through a sieve, reserving the milk and discarding the leaves for compost. Pour the liquid back into the pan and add the zest and honey. Begin to heat over low heat, whisking constantly. Add the chlorophyll at this stage if you want it to be a bright green. Slowly sprinkle in the cornstarch, whisking constantly, until it begins to get very thick. Remove from the heat and place in the refrigerator until it thickens and cools completely.

Spoon a teaspoon of the curd in the center of each cookie. If you have leftover curd, I would recommend saving it to eat with yogurt of your choice, spread on toast, or freeze for later use.

# BILBERRY/HUCKLEBERRY & ANISE HYSSOP MINI GALETTES

**MAKES 7 OR 8 INDIVIDUAL GALETTES, OR 1 LARGE GALETTE**

I have visceral memories of harvesting berries with my grandmother as the sunrise skimmed the backyard, every third berry a reward, before folding them into lemony, sweet batter or topping our morning porridge. These mini galettes are an ode to those memories, a welcome treat at the end of a long harvest day.

August marks the beginning of the bilberry harvest across many places in the world. These sparkling little red to deep blue globes—known by myriad other common names, including huckleberry—hang down from sprawling green ground cover or bushes. They are a burst of fresh blueberry flavor and combine perfectly with this lightly sweet and buttery, rustic galette.

» **SIMPLE SWAP** These galettes can be made with any berries you have available.

1 tablespoon ground flaxseeds plus 3 tablespoons water, or 1 large egg, whisked

¾ cup oat flour or sorghum flour

½ cup sweet (glutinous) white rice flour (do not use plain white rice flour)

½ cup plus 3 tablespoons almond flour or any nut or seed flour

3 tablespoons tapioca flour

2 tablespoons tapioca starch

1 teaspoon baking powder

½ teaspoon baking soda

1 teaspoon dried or fresh anise hyssop, lavender, or culinary sage

1 tablespoon coconut sugar

½ teaspoon finely ground salt

5 tablespoons butter of your choice, cold

2 tablespoons milk of your choice

2 cups bilberries/huckleberries, or berries of your choice

¼ cup maple or coconut sugar, or other sugar

1 teaspoon freshly squeezed lime juice

Oat or sorghum flour for dusting

If using, make a flax egg by combining the flax and water in a small bowl and mixing well. Let it sit for 5 minutes.

Make the crust: Combine the almond flour, tapioca flour, tapioca starch, baking powder, baking soda, anise hyssop, coconut sugar, and salt in a food processor and pulse a few times until well incorporated.

Now add 3 tablespoons of the butter, the flax egg (or whisked egg, if using), and the milk and pulse until everything is incorporated and coming together in a ball.

Remove the dough ball from the food processor and divide it into seven or eight equal-size balls. Alternatively, you can make one large galette by using all the dough.

Prepare the berry mixture by combining the berries, maple sugar, and lime juice in a medium bowl and gently mixing with a spoon. Flour a clean, dry surface with oat or sorghum flour and preheat the oven to 350°F. Line a baking sheet with parchment paper.

Roll out the balls of dough so that each forms a rough disk, ¼ to ½ inches thick. This doesn't have to be a perfect circle. Place about ¼ cup of the berry mixture in the center of each dough circle, leaving a bare margin around the edges of the dough. From the remaining 2 tablespoons of butter, add a small piece of butter on top of the berries. Fold the edges of the dough inward around the berry mixture, leaving a large portion of the berries exposed in the center. Repeat this process with each of your dough balls and transfer the galettes to the parchment-lined baking sheet. If making a single galette, roll out the dough to ¼ to ½ inch thick, top evenly with the berry mixture, and dot with the butter. Brush the crust with the flax or egg wash, or bake as is for 15 to 20 minutes. Remove the galettes from the oven when they are golden brown, allow them to cool slightly, and enjoy warm.

# WILD MINT & ANISE HYSSOP CHOCOLATE O'S

**MAKES ABOUT 12 SANDWICH COOKIES**

Oreos are a nostalgic favorite cookie from childhood, and I was inspired to re-create them with this melt-in-your-mouth, slightly more nutritious version. Summer plants from the forest and garden—anise hyssop and wild or river mint—are combined for a light, cooling sandwich cookie. Anise hyssop has a flavor of light cinnamon and its namesake, anise. Wild mint has a striking peppermint scent and flavor—it's a plant you often smell before you see it on a trail. With the combination of cooling and digestive plants, this is the perfect treat for a hot day.

» **SIMPLE SWAP** Substitute regular mint for the wild mint and anise hyssop, or use an extra ½ teaspoon of culinary peppermint flavor/oil for the creamy center in place of the wild mint and anise hyssop.

## COOKIES

1 tablespoon ground flaxseeds plus 3 tablespoons water, or 1 large egg, whisked

1⅓ cups blanched almond or hazelnut flour

½ cup unsweetened cocoa powder

½ teaspoon baking soda

½ teaspoon sea salt

½ cup monk fruit granulated sugar, or cane or coconut sugar

5½ tablespoons coconut oil, melted, or butter of your choice, melted

Make the cookies: Preheat your oven to 350°F and line a baking sheet with parchment paper. Prepare your flax egg by mixing together the flaxseeds and water in a small bowl and allowing it to sit for 10 minutes. Combine the almond flour, cocoa powder, baking soda, salt, and sugar in a large bowl and whisk together well. Stir in the melted coconut oil and flax egg (or whisked egg, if using) until well incorporated. Form the dough into a log and wrap in parchment paper. Place the dough in the freezer for about 10 minutes.

Remove the dough from the freezer, unwrap it, and roll it out between two pieces of parchment paper until ¼ to ½ inch thick. Use a cookie cutter to cut about 2-inch disks from the dough and place them ½ inch apart on your prepared baking sheet. You should have 24 disks. Place the baking sheet in the freezer for 5 minutes.

Remove the baking sheet from the freezer and bake the cookies for 9 to 10 minutes, or until lightly crisp. They won't be crispy all the way until they cool down, so remove from the oven and let cool on the baking sheet and then transfer them to a plate to be filled.

**FILLING**

4 tablespoons butter of your choice (I use Miyokos cultured vegan butter)

½ to 1 cup powdered monk fruit sugar, or cane or coconut powdered sugar

1 tablespoon very finely chopped fresh peppermint

1 generous teaspoon very finely chopped fresh anise hyssop or additional mint leaves

1½ teaspoons pure vanilla extract

½ teaspoon culinary peppermint-flavor oil

1 dropperful of liquid chlorophyll or green food dye for color

Sprinkle of salt

While the cookies cool, whip the butter and powdered sugar together in a stand mixer fitted with the paddle attachment, starting slowly, then increasing the speed to high as the sugar incorporates into the butter. Or in a medium bowl, using a hand mixer, beat until creamy. Then, add the peppermint, anise hyssop, vanilla, mint oil, chlorophyll, and salt and mix until smooth and creamy.

Pipe or spread the frosting onto an overturned cooled cookie and sandwich it with another cooled cookie. Repeat until all your cookies are filled. Arrange on a plate to serve.

# ROSE PETAL DREAMSICLES WITH CHOCOLATE SHELL

**MAKES 4 ICE-CREAM POPS**

These are a creamy, lightly sweet treat infused with the magic of rose petals, enrobed in chocolate. I was daydreaming of the chocolate-shelled ice creams I ate as a kid, and added the heart-opening wild rose, the balance of crunchy pistachios, and energizing nettle seeds. Roses are a cooling, astringent flower, high in beneficial tannins, well matched with the crisp bite of dark chocolate and the sweetness of coconut cream.

### ICE CREAM

One 13.5-ounce can full-fat coconut milk

1 tablespoon honey or sweetener of your choice

1½ tablespoons rose petal powder

½ teaspoon pure vanilla extract

1 tablespoon beet juice (optional, for color)

### CHOCOLATE SHELL

2 tablespoons pistachios, chopped

½ teaspoon nettle seeds

Sprinkle of dried rose petals

½ cup chopped 72% dark chocolate of your choice

2 tablespoons coconut oil

**NOTE**  You can buy powdered rose petals or grind up your own dried rose petals in a coffee or spice grinder.

Make the ice cream: Heat the coconut milk in a small saucepan over medium heat. Whisk in the honey and turn off the heat, making sure the sweetener is fully dissolved. Once the honey is dissolved, add the rose powder and vanilla, whisking until mixed well. Stir in the beet juice (if using). Pour the milk mixture into ice pop molds and freeze until solidly frozen, 1 to 2 hours. Make sure you have space in your freezer to set a large plate level to refreeze the pops when coated with chocolate.

Once the ice cream is frozen, line a plate with parchment and begin to prep the chocolate shells: Ready your pistachios, seeds, and rose petals for decorating the outside, because the shells will harden quickly. Then, make a double boiler: Half-fill a medium or small saucepan with water and bring to a low boil. Place a heat-safe medium bowl on top, making sure the bowl is not touching the water. Combine the chocolate and coconut oil in the bowl and stir until melted. Remove the bowl from the saucepan.

Remove one pop at a time from the freezer and use a large spoon to pour the melted chocolate over it. Quickly sprinkle with the pistachios and other toppings, place the pop on your parchment-lined plate, and place the plate in the freezer. Repeat this step as you make each pop. Let the pops rest in the freezer for at least 10 minutes to harden the shells and ice cream before you enjoy them.

If you have extra chocolate, you can save it in the refrigerator for up to a month and reheat it for a later batch of pops.

# WILD ROSE SYRUP GRANITAS

Wild rose syrup is a staple in my kitchen, offering a dreamy escape to a field of wild roses with every pour over snow or spoonful stirred into drinks. Rose syrup is light and lends itself beautifully to a variety of desserts and drinks.

Granitas are a story of place woven into food, originally made from snow that was gathered on Mt. Etna, Sicily. The snow was carried down the volcano, stored in nivieri, stone recesses that acted as a natural freezer, and used for granitas in the hot summer. Sicilian food and history is a winding road, with many Arabic and African foods at its roots. I created this recipe for a Sicilian farm dinner after an ancestral journey and research trip there in 2018. To make it at home, I collect snow in winter or spring, and save it in my freezer for summer.

❀ **FORAGER'S NOTE** As you collect your rose petals, leave the bud behind so the rose hip can still form.

## ROSE SYRUP

2 cups water

2 cups organic cane sugar or sweetener of your choice

4 cups wild rose petals (unsprayed, and most fragrant rose you can find)

## GRANITAS

Clean snow, fresh or frozen, about ½ cup per serving (optional)

A sprinkle of rose petal powder (optional)

Make the rose syrup: Combine the water and sugar in a large pot and heat, uncovered, over medium-high heat until the sugar is dissolved and the water comes to a boil. Lower the heat to a simmer, add the rose petals, cover, and cook gently for 5 minutes. Turn off the heat and let the mixture steep for 2 hours.

Strain the rose syrup into a glass jar and refrigerate for 2 to 3 weeks, or freeze and thaw as needed.

Make your granitas: Remove any gathered snow from your freezer and blend it in a food processor to fluff it back up. Pour over the rose syrup until it reaches your desired sweetness. Alternatively, if you don't have snow, add water to the rose syrup to your desired sweetness, mix, and freeze for a few hours. Then, place the frozen rose syrup ice in a blender or food processor and break it up until it resembles a snow cone consistency. Enjoy as is, or top with more syrup to taste, plus a sprinkle of rose petal powder.

# WILD ROSE & STRAWBERRY "MILK"

**SERVES 2**

Fresh strawberries picked in the mountains, fields, or forest are one of the great joys of summer. Strawberries are a member of the rose plant family, and the scent and flavor of these two ingredients together makes for a celebratory, cooling summer drink. Oats are soothing to the nervous system, and blended with the rose and strawberry, you'll have the fixings for undiluted relaxation.

» **SIMPLE SWAPS** Use any kind of milk you want for this recipe. If you don't have access to roses, you can try this recipe with a drop of rosewater or 2 teaspoons of finely powdered, dried rose petals.

2¾ cups oat milk or any milk of
    your choice

1 cup wild or regular strawberries

¼ cup fresh rose petals

3 tablespoons pure maple
    syrup or honey

¼ teaspoon black or green
    cardamom, ground to a
    fine powder

¼ teaspoon sea salt

Pinch of ground cinnamon

Combine all the ingredients in a blender, and blend on high speed until completely mixed. Serve over flower-filled ice cubes and sprinkled with dried rose petals, or gently warm the milk for a rosy latte.

# CORN SILK TEA

**MAKES 1 QUART**

Corn silk tea is a delicate, refreshing, naturally sweet tea, containing large amounts of B vitamins and vitamins C, E, and K, that is a treasured remedy for kidneys and bladder ailments across the world. Corn silk is the pollinated lifeline out of a husk of corn, each silky thread creating a kernel.

I started drinking corn silk tea when I began growing corn many years ago in Española, New Mexico. I had been gifted with a certain variety of corn, now known as Rainbow or Glass Gem corn. Rainbow corn emerged—or rather reemerged—under the watchful tending of Carl Barnes, a Cherokee and Scottish-Irish farmer from Oklahoma who dedicated his later life to bringing back lost corn varieties and sharing them with the tribes from whom they were stolen or lost. The corn was gifted to me by a student of Carl's, a prolific seed saver named Greg Schoen who lived in the Gila wilderness of southern New Mexico. Corn silk tea is a perfect, cooling summer drink that I love to make with the freshly harvested silks on hot days, or with dried silk other times of the year.

✤ **FORAGER'S NOTE**  To harvest the silk of corn, peel back the outer leaves of a fresh corn cob and save the delicate threads inside. Gently dry the threads on a clean cotton towel to save for later, or you can enjoy them fresh. Any variety of corn can be used.

¼ cup to a handful of corn silk from any fresh corn (sweet corn, flint, popping, etc.)

Place your corn silk in a large jar. Heat enough water in a kettle or saucepan that you can cover the corn silk in your jar. It should be around 100°F. Seal the jar and infuse overnight in the refrigerator for a refreshing tea the next day, or strain and drink it hot after 10 minutes.

# FERMENTED FIREWEED TEA/IVAN CHAI

**MAKES 1 CUP DRIED TEA**

Fermented fireweed tea, known as Ivan chai, tastes remarkably like traditional black tea. It's a fermented 12th-century recipe from Russia steeped in folklore and stories. Rosebay willowherb, known as fireweed, is a phoenix plant, often rising up from the ashes of a recent forest fire. In World War II, it was spotted emerging from the rubble of bombed buildings, hence its other common name, bombweed. Pushing up in giant spikes of magenta flowers with willowlike leaves, this plant starts the process of healing land by rooting in, breaking up soil, bringing nutrients, and setting the stage for the succession of plants and trees to follow. The young shoots can be eaten, similar to asparagus, but this plant shines as a fermented tea with rich vanilla notes. In addition to the storied background of this drink, the rolled, fermented leaves of fireweed are naturally caffeine-free and energizing, rich in B vitamins, vitamin C, tannins, and magnesium and other minerals.

✤ **FORAGER'S NOTE**  Using a foraging or plant identification book, make sure you are harvesting correctly, and gather the leaves of rosebay willowherb. You can harvest just the top or bottom leaves off several stalks, leaving many of the leaves and most of the flowers on the stalks to bloom and feed the pollinators.

---

2 tablespoons rosebay
  willowherb flowers

4 to 6 cups rosebay
  willowherb leaves

Lay the leaves and flowers, in a single layer, on a clean towel when you get home from foraging, leaving the flowers out to dry completely and letting the leaves wilt for 6 to 10 hours, depending on the moisture in the air. In very dry locations, you will need less time for wilting. After wilting, begin rolling the leaves between your fingers and palms until they are completely bruised and seep green. Then, twist them into small bundles. Place the rolled leaves in a ceramic or clay bowl and cover with a damp cloth; don't completely seal the vessel, allowing some oxygen into the bowl. Wait 24 to 36 hours for the leaves to ferment and deepen in color. The smell will change from bright green and grassy to a deep earthy, with black tea and vanilla scents. Do not forget the leaves at this stage as they can mold quickly.

Once the leaves have fermented, set a dehydrator to low heat and place the leaves inside. Dehydrate the leaves until they are completely dry. If you don't have a dehydrator, you can spread the leaves out in a single layer on a baking sheet and set them out for several days in a dry, dark place with good air circulation until they are completely dry. Move them daily, flipping them over so they do not mold, and so they dry evenly.

Once completely dried, place the leaves in a sealed and labeled jar with the flowers and enjoy all year. To make a tea, pinch a bundle of 1 to 2 teaspoons into a cup or tea strainer, and pour 8 to 10 ounces of boiling water over the top. Steep for 5 to 10 minutes, then stir in the sweetener of your choice.

# FALL

# ADAPTOGENIC SELKIE SIPPING BROTH

**MAKES 16 MUGS, OR 1 MUG PLUS LEFTOVER BROTH**

When I make a broth, it is an answer to what I or whoever is going to drink it needs most in the moment. Stirring the pot, I feel guided to add layers of seaweed, gathered roots, greens, and alliums, alchemizing to become a sip of the sea and the mountains, the perfect balance. Nearly all my ancestors were coastal peoples, and simmering this brew in gallon measure on my stove, I imagine them smiling over my shoulder, whispering in my ear to add another handful of nettles or sprig of rosemary.

This is my favorite nutrient-dense, mineral-rich broth for building immunity, reducing inflammation, and enjoying in the morning with a spoonful of miso or as the foundation for soup or stew. Make it on your stovetop or in a slow cooker. This is an easy way to get your herbs and mushrooms in a delicious drink. I use this broth as a base for many soup recipes; it has a deep flavor and works great with the nettle soup on page 51 and the lentil dal on page 189.

## BASIC BROTH

16 cups water

1 large onion, chopped in half

½ large acorn or other orange winter squash, roasted in the oven, seeds removed, skin-on

1 celery stalk, chopped

3 cups (6 or more strips) seaweed (kombu, alaria, digitata kelp)

2 cups dried mushrooms, or 4 cups fresh (shiitake, porcini, lion's mane)

¼ cup calendula flowers

½ cup dried nettle leaf, or 2 cups fresh

3 to 4 garlic cloves

1 tablespoon grated fresh ginger

4 thyme sprigs, or 2 teaspoons dried

2 rosemary sprigs, or 1 teaspoon dried

1 to 2 sprigs oregano or wild oregano, Monarda fistulosa, or 1 teaspoon dried

1 tablespoon dried culinary sage

1 teaspoon salt, or more to taste

## OPTIONAL

1 to 2 tablespoons grated fresh turmeric root, or 1 tablespoon powdered

1 to 2 tablespoons dried burdock root, or 1 fresh root, chopped

¼ cup fresh dandelion leaf, or 2 tablespoons dried

1 to 2 tablespoons dandelion root (not roasted)

1 to 2 tablespoons dried astragalus root

## GARNISH (PER MUG, AT TIME OF SERVING)

Squeeze of lemon juice or 1 tablespoon miso

Make the basic broth: Combine all the basic broth ingredients, adding any of the optional ingredients according to your preference, in a large pot and simmer over very low heat for 3 to 4 hours. You can also make this using a slow cooker; set on LOW, cooking for 3 to 4 hours, or overnight.

Once the mixture has simmered, strain the broth, pressing as much of it as possible through a mesh sieve set over a large bowl or container, reserving the liquid. Add salt to taste and ladle the broth into a mug. Add a squeeze of lemon or a tablespoon of miso to your mug, stirring to dissolve the miso. Don't simmer or boil the miso as the enzymes in miso are alive and can't survive the heat.

**NOTE** Many of the dried herbs, flowers, and mushrooms can be purchased online in bulk. If you aren't able to find all the ingredients, make a broth with what you have available. Let this serve as a guide, but enjoy with the ingredients you have on hand. Any mushrooms will work, and porcini will give the broth an amazing flavor. If using a combination of mushrooms, know that certain mushrooms, such as reishi and sometimes lion's mane, have a more bitter flavor. Add a smaller amount of these mushrooms if you are sensitive to bitter flavors.

# ROASTED KALE SALAD WITH BLACK SESAME DRESSING

**SERVES 4**

This is a flavorful, nutrient-dense roasted fall harvest salad with a rainbow of colorful vegetables. It is warming with oven-toasted ribbons of fresh kale and toasted coconut, fresh pomegranate seeds, and a creamy black sesame dressing.

## SALAD

2 large bunches lacinato (dinosaur) kale, stripped from the stems and torn into 2-inch pieces

¼ cup of unsweetened large-flake coconut

¼ cup toasted sesame oil

2 tablespoons soy sauce

2 to 3 purple carrots, shredded finely

Seeds from ½ pomegranate

¼ cup yellow or red cherry tomatoes

¼ cup sliced purple daikon radish, cut in thin rounds

2 tablespoons pickled radish or pickled purple cabbage

Edible flowers: sweet alyssum, calendula, gem marigolds, or radish flowers

## BLACK SESAME DRESSING

3 tablespoons black sesame seeds

¼ cup olive oil

¼ cup water

Zest and juice of 1 lime

2 tablespoons soy sauce

1 tablespoon pure maple syrup

Make the salad: Preheat the oven to 425°F. Evenly spread the torn kale and flaked coconut on two large baking sheets. Pour half of the toasted sesame oil and soy sauce over one baking sheet, and half over the other. Use your hands to toss the kale and coconut in the oil and soy sauce, coating evenly, and put both sheets in the oven. Roast for 10 to 20 minutes, checking every 5 to 7 minutes to turn the kale and coconut over with a large spoon. Once the kale has reduced in size and is beginning to get some brown or crisped edges, pull out both pans.

While the pans cool, make your dressing: Lightly toast the black sesame seeds in a small, dry skillet over medium-high heat, then transfer to a blender. Add the rest of the dressing ingredients to the blender and blend on high speed until smooth.

Transfer the roasted kale and coconut to a large salad bowl. Starting from the center, add a pile of shredded carrot, sprinkle with the pomegranate seeds, add the tomatoes and the purple daikon rounds, and place the brightly colored pickle on top of the carrots in the center.

Drizzle with the toasted black sesame dressing and garnish with the flowers. Save whatever dressing you don't use for up to 2 weeks in the refrigerator.

# TATAKI GOBO (BURDOCK ROOT)

**SERVES 2**

This is a grounding dish I start craving in late summer and early fall, waiting until after the first frost to harvest this beloved root. Burdock root has been used as a food and medicine for hundreds of years in North America, China, and Japan, and in Ayurvedic medicine. Burdock root is for sale in grocery stores in many places now, and it is also classified as a weed in many areas, making it a great plant to forage.

Burdock has a light artichoke flavor and, coupled with a warm sesame dressing, it makes an amazing seasonal salad. Tataki gobo is a traditional Japanese pounded burdock salad made to symbolize good luck and stability for the home and family.

1 large burdock root, about 12 inches long, or 2 smaller roots, about 6 inches long, all about 1 inch in diameter

2 to 3 tablespoons white sesame seeds

1 tablespoon mirin, or ¼ teaspoon coconut sugar mixed with 1 tablespoon hard cider or white wine

1 to 2 teaspoons rice vinegar or cider vinegar

1 tablespoon soy sauce

Black sesame seeds for sprinkling (optional)

Gently scrape the fine layer of skin off your burdock root with the back of a knife. Refrain from peeling too deeply, as it will remove a lot of the root's light artichoke/nutty flavor. Place the scraped root in a bowl of water with 2 tablespoons of vinegar for at least 5 minutes, to prevent oxidation.

Toast the white sesame seeds in a small, dry skillet until golden and fragrant, stirring continuously. Turn off the heat and set the sesame seeds aside. Bring a pot of water to a boil and add the whole burdock root to the water. Let boil for 10 to 13 minutes, until softened.

While the burdock cooks, prepare the sauce: If you have a mortar and pestle, add the sesame seeds and grind them until they are becoming fine, but still have some whole sesame seeds mixed throughout. Alternatively, use a food processor, pulsing carefully to avoid overblending. Transfer the seeds to a small bowl, add the mirin, vinegar, and soy sauce and stir to incorporate.

Remove the burdock from the pot, and while hot, cut it lengthwise into four 4-inch pieces. Then, hit it with a rolling pin until it is smashed up but still holding together. This breaks up the fibers.

Place the smashed roots in a separate bowl and pour the sauce over them. Sprinkle with black sesame seeds or sprinkle with more toasted white sesame seeds and eat warm or cold.

# ROASTED SQUASH & NETTLE TOM KHA

**SERVES 4 TO 6**

I learned to make this traditional soup in Thailand, and this version omits the chicken (gai) and adds winter squash and the second fall cutting of nettles. The flavors of this soup are lightly spicy from the chile, sour from the lime and sweet and creamy with the addition of coconut milk. It's an excellent rainy day soup, warming from the inside out. Many of the ingredients, such as galangal, lime leaves, and lemongrass are both culinary and medicinal plants, used to support the immune system, reduce inflammation, and balance blood sugar.

✻ **FORAGER'S NOTE** Nettles will return in the cool weather of fall, if they have been cut in spring or summer. When harvesting nettles, remove only the tops of the plants in spring and summer, tending them gently so they return vigorously in fall. Always practice ethical harvesting by leaving plenty to go to seed and only harvesting from abundant patches.

» **SIMPLE SWAPS** Substitute spinach for nettles and fresh cilantro leaf for coriander berries. Substitute any spicy pepper for Thai spicy pepper. If you cannot find galangal, you can substitute ginger, but it will be a different flavor profile.

1 whole acorn squash

Olive oil for rubbing

4 cups vegetable or chicken stock

2 lemongrass stalks, bruised with the back of a knife

5 to 7 slices galangal

4 garlic cloves, smashed

7 makrut lime leaves, or the zest of 1 to 2 limes

2 cups full-fat coconut milk or coconut cream

4 cups shiitake, oyster, or button mushrooms, chopped

2 teaspoons finely chopped Thai chiles, such as bird's-eye; add more or less to taste

4 to 5 shallots, chopped

1 tablespoon coconut sugar

Preheat the oven to 400°F. Place the acorn squash in a baking dish and, using a knife, poke 3 or 4 holes in it, all around the outside. Rub with olive oil and bake for 35 minutes, or until it is cooked through. Cut it open and scoop out the seeds.

Combine the stock, lemongrass, galangal, garlic, and lime leaves in a large pot over medium heat and simmer for 15 minutes. Remove and discard all the aromatics from the stock and then stir in the coconut milk. Stir in the mushrooms, Thai chile, shallots, coconut sugar, and fish sauce and simmer for another 5 minutes.

Stir in the nettle leaf and let simmer while you scoop spoonfuls of the squash into the soup, about 1 tablespoon each time. Simmer for a few minutes to warm the squash.

4 to 5 tablespoons fish sauce or vegan fish sauce

1 cup fresh nettle leaf

5 tablespoons freshly squeezed lime juice

2 tablespoons coriander berries, or ¼ cup fresh cilantro

5 or 6 nasturtium flowers for garnish

Thai basil leaves for garnish

If you are using lime zest instead of leaves, add that now with the lime juice, adjusting the amount to taste. Taste the broth and add more sweet, spicy, or salty flavors as needed. Turn off the heat. Stir in the coriander berries or cilantro and ladle into bowls. Garnish with spicy-sweet nasturtium flowers and Thai basil.

# EARLY FALL VEGETABLE STEW

**SERVES 4 TO 6**

A combination of warming spices like turmeric and thyme, and the last summer squash, beans, and tomatoes make this the perfect late summer and early fall stew. With the shift in seasons, the focus turns to building up the immune system and adding nourishing, hearty roots and greens to regular meals.

3 tablespoons olive oil

2 garlic cloves, chopped

1 large yellow onion, chopped

10 cups tomatoes, chopped loosely, or three 28-ounce cans crushed tomatoes

1½ teaspoons sea salt, plus more to taste

1 tablespoon turmeric powder

1 tablespoon ground cumin

4 to 6 cups vegetable broth or water, or more as needed

1½ cups cooked or one 15-ounce can chickpeas, drained, 1 cup cooking liquid reserved

1½ cups cooked, or one 15-ounce can kidney beans, drained and rinsed

3 small to medium zucchini

One 6-inch or two 10-inch burdock roots, peeled and sliced in thin rounds

2 large carrots, chopped

4 medium potatoes, chopped loosely in 1-inch cubes

1 cup peeled and chopped orange winter squash (acorn, delicata, etc.)

3 tablespoons fresh thyme, or 2 teaspoons dried

2 to 3 cups fresh greens (nettles, chard, spinach), chopped finely

Lemon zest

Heat the oil in a large pot over medium heat, then add the garlic and cook for 2 minutes, or until fragrant. Stir in the onion and cook until translucent. Stir the tomatoes into the pot. Then, sprinkle in the salt, turmeric, and cumin. Cook until the tomatoes begin to "melt" and soften.

Add the broth or water, and then the chickpeas with their reserved liquid, kidney beans, zucchini, burdock roots, carrots, potatoes, and squash. Cover and simmer until the potatoes, burdock, and carrots soften, about 15 minutes. Sprinkle in the fresh thyme and greens and stir well; cook for another 5 minutes. Finish with lemon zest.

Serve on top of quinoa, pasta, couscous, or rice. Alternatively, you can serve it with a bread of your choice, or enjoy the stew on its own.

# NETTLE GNOCCHI WITH BLACK KALE PESTO

**SERVES 4**

This gnocchi recipe comes from the love of nettles and a desire to deeply nourish the body as the weather shifts. Nettles are my favorite plant, and I work with them in all seasons from the seeds to the leaves and roots. In this recipe, dried and powdered nettles are used along with a few fresh leaves wrapped onto the gnocchi.

Black kale, cavolo nero in Italian, makes for a delicious sauce this time of year, as brassicas love the cold weather of fall and become sweeter as the temperature drops. At a time when basil is getting harder to find fresh, this is a great option for a fresh green sauce. It can be made with all kale if basil is not available.

2 cups peeled and chopped Yukon
    Gold potatoes

¼ cup dried nettle powder

½ cup tapioca flour

1 tablespoon coconut flour

¼ teaspoon baking soda

¼ teaspoon sea salt

1 large egg, whisked (see notes)

3 dropperfuls liquid chlorophyll
    (optional for color)

5 to 10 fresh nettle
    leaves (optional)

2 to 3 tablespoons olive oil
    for cooking

1 recipe Black Kale Pesto
    (recipe follows)

Toasted pine nuts for sprinkling

Bring water to a boil in a large pot and add the potato chunks. Boil the potatoes until just soft, then drain. Transfer the potatoes to a large bowl and mash with a potato masher or large fork. Add the nettle powder, flours, baking soda, salt, egg, and chlorophyll (if using) to the potatoes and incorporate, using the potato masher or a large fork. The dough should be mostly smooth.

Form the gnocchi by gathering about 2 teaspoons of dough at a time and using your hands to shape it roughly into an oval form. Repeat this process until you've shaped all the dough. Add a fresh nettle leaf to the top of some of the gnocchi and mold a bit of the dough around the leaf to keep it in place. For the rest of the gnocchi, press the back of a fork on the top to make grooves, or use a gnocchi roller if you have one. Transfer all the gnocchi to a baking sheet.

You can make the gnocchi ahead of time, up to 2 days, and store them in the refrigerator until you are ready to cook, or you can bake them right away.

To bake, preheat the oven to 350°F. Line a baking sheet with parchment paper. Have a bowl of warm water with a little olive oil next to you for dipping your hands and the fork into, so the dough doesn't stick.

*continued »*

**NOTES** You can use an egg substitute, such as flax, for the egg, or add 2 to 3 tablespoons of water to the batter; it will be slightly different in texture. The nettle powder for this recipe can be made from scratch by blending dried nettles in an electric coffee grinder. Sift out the stems before adding to the potatoes.

Bake the gnocchi for 7 minutes, then remove them from the oven. Heat the olive oil in a large skillet over medium heat. Then, add the gnocchi to the skillet and cook for 2 to 3 minutes on both sides. Remove from the heat. Add the Black Kale Pesto and pine nuts to serve.

# BLACK KALE PESTO

**SERVES 4 TO 6**

1 bunch lacinato (dinosaur) or green kale (about 1½ cups leaves), torn off the stems and chopped thinly

½ cup basil leaves

1½ tablespoons unsalted, raw pumpkin seeds

3 to 4 garlic cloves, chopped

¼ teaspoon sea salt, plus more to taste

½ cup olive oil, plus more as needed

Squeeze of lemon juice

Bring a pot of water to a boil and blanch the kale leaves for 2 minutes in the water. Drain and then cool immediately under running water or in a bowl with ice. Transfer the kale to a food processor and add the basil, pumpkin seeds, garlic, salt, olive oil, and lemon juice. Pulse lightly until the greens, oil, and pumpkin seeds are mixed well, but don't puree. Taste and add more salt, lemon juice, or olive oil as needed. Scoop onto the gnocchi, or eat with breakfast, on toast, or use as a dip.

# PORCINI & OAT PASTA WITH PORCINI MUSHROOM SAUCE

**SERVES 4**

I love to use mushroom powders in a variety of ways, most of all, incorporated into this delicious homemade pasta. The umami porcini powder gives the pasta an extra lift, but if you are unable to find or make a mushroom powder, it can be left out and the dish will be equally delicious. Porcini mushrooms with the flavorful herb nepitella (*Calamintha nepeta*, also known as calamint) is a traditional combination in Italy, and oregano is a close relative that will work in its place.

» **SIMPLE SWAPS** Substitute more oat flour in place of the porcini powder. For the sauce, porcini can be replaced with any other mushroom. Nepitella can be replaced with oregano, or a combination of oregano and other herbs, such as mint, parsley, and thyme.

*continued »*

2 cups oat flour, plus more
for dusting

2 tablespoons ground porcini
mushroom powder

2 large eggs, beaten or
2 tablespoons psyllium husk
powder and ¼ cup water

1 to 2 tablespoons olive oil, plus
more as needed

1 recipe Porcini Mushroom Sauce
(recipe follows)

**NOTE** You can add a little
xanthan gum or tapioca starch
to the batter to increase the
elasticity of the dough.

Whisk together the oat flour and porcini powder in a bowl.
Transfer the mixture to a clean work surface and make a little
volcano of the flour, with a depression in the center. Add the eggs
to the center and begin to mix them with a fork, incorporating
the flour as you go. Add the olive oil, using 1 tablespoon at a time,
incorporating more as needed. Knead the dough until it comes
together completely and feels somewhat soft.

Flour a surface with oat flour and cut the dough in half.
Keep in mind that gluten-free pasta is very different from its
gluten counterpart. It does not have the same elasticity, so it
can sometimes get dry or crumbly while working it. Keep a
little water in a bowl on your rolling space to add moisture
when needed.

Use a rolling pin to roll out one portion of the dough as thinly as
possible—the thinner the better; the thinnest pasta will still bulk
up when cooked. You can keep rolling out the dough this way.
But if you have a pasta machine, once you create a relatively thin
piece of dough, you can roll the pasta in sheets by starting on the
largest setting and working your way to the thinnest setting. Cut
the pasta into ½-inch strips for a pappardelle-style noodle, using a
sharp knife, or use a pasta maker to cut the noodles. Repeat with
the second portion of dough.

The pasta dough can be made ahead of time, wrapped up very
tight, and kept in an airtight container for a few days, but it will
dry out quickly if exposed to the air. When you're ready to cook,
bring a large pot of water to a boil and salt it to the level of ocean
water, about ¼ cup for 6 quarts of water. Boil the pasta for 3 to
5 minutes, then drain, reserving ¾ cup of the cooking water for
the sauce and discarding the rest.

Add the cooked pasta into the porcini mushroom sauce and
toss to coat the pasta. Top with fresh herbs, plus dairy or
dairy-free Parmesan.

# PORCINI MUSHROOM SAUCE

**SERVES 4**

3 tablespoons olive oil

2 garlic cloves, smashed

4 cups porcini
mushrooms, chopped

6 ounces dry white wine

3 tablespoons fresh nepitella

Sea salt

¾ cup salted pasta cooking water

2 tablespoons butter of
your choice

Heat the olive oil in a heavy-bottomed pot over medium heat and add the garlic. As it begins to release its aroma, add the mushrooms. Cook the mushrooms for 5 minutes, or until they just begin to turn golden. Now, add the wine and nepitella and cook until the wine evaporates.

Lower the heat and add salt to taste. Cook for 12 minutes, stirring occasionally. Add the pasta water and butter and continue to cook over low heat until glossy.

# NETTLE "EVERYTHING" BAGELS

### MAKES 10 TO 12 MEDIUM-SIZE BAGELS OR 6 TO 8 LARGER ONES

Bagels were one of the foods I missed the most when I had to stop eating gluten, so I created this gluten-free, vegan option that is very different from the New York City favorite but has a great flavor. Try it with Forager's Everything Salt Blend (page 229) and a generous spread of a cream cheese of your choice.

» SIMPLE SWAPS Use spinach in place of nettles. The almond flour could be replaced with hazelnut, but it will have a stronger flavor.

3 cups almond flour

1 cup tapioca flour or starch

2 teaspoons baking powder

1 teaspoon sea salt

2 cups fresh nettles

⅓ plus ¼ cup water

2 tablespoons cider vinegar

2 tablespoons pure maple
    syrup or honey

1 large egg whisked, or equivalent
    amount egg replacer
    for brushing

Forager's Everything Salt
    Blend (page 229) or a
    store-bought version

Preheat the oven to 350°F and line a baking pan with parchment paper or a silicone baking mat. Fill a large pot with water and bring to a very gentle boil. Whisk together the almond flour, tapioca flour, baking powder, and salt in a medium bowl. Process the nettles in a food processor until they are very fine.

Add the processed nettles, water, vinegar, and maple syrup to the flour mixture and mix well until they are all incorporated and the dough feels smooth. Add more water if it feels at all dry.

Wet your hands, then mold and divide the dough equally into 10 to 12 balls, or 6 to 8 balls for larger bagels. Take a ball in your hand and poke a hole in the center with your thumb. Sculpt it from the center so it forms a ring. Add the bagel to the gently boiling water. It should float up, and the water will get doughy. Remove the bagel as soon as it floats. Place the boiled bagel on your cookie sheet and repeat one bagel at a time, with all the remaining dough.

Place the bagels on the prepared baking pan and bake for 10 minutes. Remove from the oven, brush each bagel with egg, and liberally sprinkle the salt blend across the top of the bagels. Now, put the pan back in the oven and bake again for around 15 minutes. These bagels will not be lofty like a regular bagel as they are grain-free, but they should start to brown and appear golden on top. Once they are golden, remove from the oven and let cool. To serve, cut in half and finish off with your favorite bagel toppings/spreads.

# WINTER SQUASH
# RAINBOW CORNBREAD

**SERVES 4 TO 8**

Corn is a favorite plant I have grown and learned from over the years. This cornbread is made with a variety I grow, a field corn that is from the Rainbow/Glass Gem variety. You can use any kind of finely ground cornmeal, blue or yellow, to make this recipe, and it works great as muffins or baked in a skillet.

2 cups fine-grind pan-toasted rainbow corn, or fine-grind blue or yellow cornmeal

¾ teaspoon baking soda

¾ teaspoon baking powder

½ teaspoon sea salt

3 tablespoons coconut oil, ghee, or butter of your choice

3 large eggs

1 tablespoon pure maple syrup

1 teaspoon cider vinegar

1½ cups coconut milk

½ cup pureed roasted winter squash or pumpkin

1 to 2 tablespoons blackstrap molasses

Preheat your oven to 425°F. Whisk together the cornmeal, baking soda, baking powder, and salt in a large bowl. Add the oil to a 10-inch skillet and place in the oven while it preheats.

Beat the eggs in a medium bowl, then stir in the maple syrup. In a smaller bowl, whisk the cider vinegar into the coconut milk, and let sit for 3 minutes. Whisk the squash into the milk mixture, then whisk that mixture into the maple syrup mixture. Finally, stir the wet mixture into the cornmeal mixture and mix well.

Remove the skillet from the oven and rotate it a few times so the oil coats the inside. Pour the batter into the hot skillet. Drizzle the molasses on the top of the batter in parallel lines, running a skewer or knife through them to feather the molasses. Bake for 15 to 20 minutes, depending on your oven. Remove the cornbread from the oven when the bread is cooked through—the top will be golden and will be firm and bouncy. Let cool for a few minutes and enjoy warm!

# SQUASH & ROASTED DANDELION ROOT GELATO

**SERVES 4 TO 6**

Roasted squash gelato is a celebration of the seasonal foraged and grown harvest at our farm and is one of the most requested fall treats in our house. As the frost settles in the morning, and the heat of late summer gives way to fall, squash and pumpkins concentrate their sugars on the vine, and dandelions push energy into their roots. Pumpkins and squash have been cultivated and enjoyed for more than 9,000 years; they are an incredible source of natural sweetness, beta-carotene, vitamins A and C, and potassium. I love the squash varieties Koginut, Blue Hubbard, or kabocha in this recipe, but any sweet and creamy squash will work. This gelato comes together easily and is perfect when sandwiched between Double Chocolate Chestnut & Yellow Dock Seed Cookies (page 150), presented on a holiday table, or served in a cone on a sunny fall day.

2 to 3 pounds winter squash or pumpkin, or 3 cups cooked or canned

1 tablespoon roasted dandelion root, powdered and sifted

¾ cup pure maple syrup

3 tablespoons coconut sugar

⅔ cup full-fat coconut milk

½ teaspoon sea salt

1 tablespoon pure vanilla extract

½ teaspoon ground cinnamon

Preheat your oven to 400°F. Poke several holes in the pumpkin or squash with a sharp knife and place on a baking sheet. Roast for about 40 minutes to 1 hour, depending on the size. Check the squash for doneness by pressing on the skin; if it gives slightly and is getting soft, remove from the oven and let cool completely.

Cut the cooled squash in half, remove the seeds, and scoop out the squash, transferring it to a high-speed blender. Sift the dandelion root through a mesh sieve and discard any chunky bits, then add the powder to the blender. Add all the remaining ingredients and blend until smooth. Refrigerate for 20 minutes, or until the mixture is completely cold.

Pour the mixture into an ice-cream maker and follow the manufacturer's instructions to churn until the gelato is creamy and frozen. If you don't have an ice-cream maker, just place the mixture in a container in the freezer and stir every 20 minutes, or until creamy and frozen.

Serve this gelato on its own, scoop into a cone, or top your favorite seasonal cookie or pie. Store in the freezer in a sealed container.

# DOUBLE CHOCOLATE CHESTNUT & YELLOW DOCK SEED COOKIES

**MAKES 12 TO 14 COOKIES**

Chocolate, chestnuts, and yellow dock seeds combine to make these delightful cookies. Yellow or curly dock, *Rumex crispus*, is often considered a weed and can be harvested all the way through winter. The seeds taste a bit like a cross between cinnamon and buckwheat, a relative of *Rumex crispus*, especially when lightly toasted and ground. Try these cookies in an ice-cream sandwich with Squash & Roasted Dandelion Root Gelato on page 148.

» **SIMPLE SWAPS** Almond flour or another nut flour can be substituted for the chestnut flour. The yellow dock seeds can be replaced with more nut flour or another seed flour.

½ cup ground yellow dock seeds

1 cup chestnut flour

1¼ cups blanched almond flour

½ teaspoon baking soda

½ teaspoon sea salt

¼ cup unsweetened cocoa powder

2 tablespoons tapioca flour or starch

¾ cup pure maple syrup

½ cup coconut oil, melted

One 3.5-ounce dark chocolate bar of your choice, cut in small chunks, or ½ cup plus 2 tablespoons dark chocolate chips of your choice

Preheat the oven to 350°F and line two baking sheets with parchment paper. Place your dock seeds on one baking sheet and roast for just 5 minutes, until they are a deeper brown color. Allow the seeds to cool and transfer them to a blender. Blend to a fine flour and then sift the powder into a bowl, discarding any chaff.

Whisk together the dock seed flour, chestnut flour, almond flour, baking soda, sea salt, cocoa powder, and tapioca flour in a large bowl. Stir in the maple syrup and melted coconut oil and mix well until everything is incorporated.

Scoop out 1 to 2 tablespoons of dough at a time and form a dough ball. Repeat this until you've used all your dough and arrange the cookie dough balls on your second prepared baking sheet. Flatten the cookies to ½ inch with the back of a spoon. Bake for 10 to 13 minutes, remove from the oven, and let cool completely before eating.

## Golden Ice-Cream Sandwiches

This recipe evolved naturally as soon as I made these cookies and the Squash & Roasted Dandelion Root Gelato (page 148).

Putting these sandwiches together is easy:

Freeze your cookies in advance, making sure you have an even number to make both sides of the sandwich. Remove the gelato from the freezer and let it warm up just enough to be able to scoop. Using a spoon, add about 2 tablespoons of ice cream to the center of one overturned cookie and sandwich the second cookie on top.

Add more gelato or ice cream around the sides of the sandwich to fill out the gaps. To smooth the outside, warm a butter knife under hot water and run it around the sandwiched ice cream. Place the ice-cream sandwiches back in the freezer so they stay solid, or eat them right away!

# DANDELION ROOT & PEANUT BUTTER COOKIES

**MAKES 12 COOKIES**

This is a simple cookie with just six ingredients, satisfying any craving for something sweet, crunchy, and a little salty. The dandelion root adds an earthy hint of coffee, loads of vitamins and minerals, prebiotic benefits, and it has been used to help stabilize blood sugar. These cookies are great with chopped chocolate pieces, but leave it out for a simple protein-rich snack or plain peanut butter cookie.

» **SIMPLE SWAP** Use any other nut or seed butter here, such as thick tahini, cashew butter, etc.

1 tablespoon ground flaxseeds plus 3 tablespoons water, or 1 large egg, beaten

1 cup crunchy or smooth peanut butter (no added oils or sugar, as this will alter the texture of the cookies)

¾ cup monk fruit granulated sugar or any other granulated sugar

2 tablespoons roasted dandelion root, powdered (see Roasted Dandelion Root "Coffee," page 163)

½ teaspoon vanilla extract

¼ cup semisweet chocolate chips or chopped chocolate of your choice

Maldon sea salt for sprinkling (optional)

Preheat the oven to 350°F, and line a baking sheet with parchment paper. Prepare your flax egg (if using) by combining the flaxseeds and water in a small bowl and allowing it to thicken for 5 minutes.

Combine all the ingredients, except the chocolate chips and salt, in a medium bowl and whisk with a fork until incorporated. Add the chocolate chips and mix well.

Form the cookies with your hands, making little balls about 1½ tablespoons in size, and pressing each cookie down into a 3-inch-diameter disk onto the prepared baking sheet. They will not spread when baking. Use the back of a fork to press lines into the cookies in one direction and then to press again across those lines, making a kind of tic-tac-toe board across the top. If using, sprinkle the top of each cookie lightly with Maldon salt.

Bake for 7 to 10 minutes, until golden, and let them cool completely before eating or they will fall apart.

# GOLDEN SQUASH PIE WITH PECAN STREUSEL

**SERVES 8 TO 10**

This recipe is a twist on the traditional pumpkin pie, incorporating a sweet and salty, crunchy streusel of pecans on a classically creamy squash or pumpkin pie. Pecans are rich in minerals, including manganese and copper, and healthy fats, aiding in the reduction of inflammation, and supporting the metabolism. Winter squash is a staple food, harvested at its sweetest and most nutritious in the late fall, and it is an excellent source of fiber and vitamins A, $B_6$, and C.

Additionally, this filling pairs wonderfully with my Go-To Gluten-Free Piecrust. The pastry has a great texture and flavor, and can be easily altered to work for savory and sweet pies, tarts, and galettes. Double the recipe to make a top and bottom crust.

## SQUASH FILLING

One 2½-pound pumpkin or winter squash

1 recipe Go-To Gluten-Free Piecrust (recipe follows)

2 tablespoons gluten-free flour blend

⅓ cup coconut sugar

½ teaspoon ground nutmeg

½ teaspoon ground cinnamon

½ teaspoon salt

1¼ cups full-fat coconut milk or heavy cream

3 large eggs

1 cup pure maple syrup

## PECAN STREUSEL

1 cup whole pecans or pieces

¼ cup coconut sugar or light brown sugar

½ teaspoon ground cinnamon

2 tablespoons tapioca flour

2 tablespoons cold butter of your choice, diced

Start your filling: Preheat your oven to 425°F. Place the whole pumpkin on a baking sheet and poke several holes in it with a knife. Roast for 30 to 45 minutes, checking after 25 minutes to see whether it is softening. Once it is soft and caves a bit to the touch, take it out and cut it in half, scooping out all the seeds, then scraping out the cooked inside. Leave the oven on.

Prepare your piecrust and have it ready, off to the side. Put the 2 cups of the roasted squash in a blender or large bowl along with the gluten-free flour, coconut sugar, nutmeg, cinnamon, salt, coconut milk, eggs, and maple syrup. Blend on high speed (using a hand blender, if necessary), until creamy and smooth. Pour the filling into the piecrust.

Bake the pie for 15 minutes at 425°F. After 15 minutes, lower the temperature to 350°F and bake for another 15 minutes while you prepare the pecan streusel.

Make the pecan streusel: Lightly toast the pecans in a dry, medium skillet over medium heat, stirring constantly, until they release their scent, 4 to 5 minutes. Remove from the heat and transfer them to a small bowl to cool slightly while you combine the coconut sugar, cinnamon, and tapioca flour in a separate small bowl. Toss the pecans in the dry mixture and then add the cold diced butter, working it in until it creates small clumps.

At the 30-minute mark, remove the pie from the oven. At this point, the pie filling should have thickened slightly, but will still be wobbly. Sprinkle the streusel mixture on top of the filling, return the pie to the oven, and bake for another 15 to 25 minutes. The piecrust should be a golden brown and the center of the pie firm but a bit wobbly; it will firm up as it cools. Remove the pie from the oven and allow it to cool on a cooling rack before slicing and enjoying.

*continued »*

# GO-TO GLUTEN-FREE PIECRUST

**MAKES ONE 9- TO 10-INCH SINGLE CRUST**

1 tablespoon ground flaxseeds plus
¼ cup water

¾ cup oat flour

½ cup sweet white rice flour

½ cup plus 3 tablespoons
almond flour

3 tablespoons tapioca
flour or starch

1 teaspoon baking powder

½ teaspoon baking soda

1 tablespoon coconut sugar

½ teaspoon salt

3 tablespoons butter of your
choice, cold, chopped

2 tablespoons milk of your choice

**NOTE** Sweet white rice
flour, also known as glutinous
white rice flour because it is
made from sticky rice, does
not contain gluten. It cannot
be replaced with regular
rice flours.

Prepare your flax egg by mixing the flaxseeds and water in a small bowl and allowing to rest for 5 minutes. Set aside.

Combine the oat flour, rice flour, almond flour, tapioca flour, baking powder, baking soda, coconut sugar, and salt in a food processor and pulse a few times until everything is incorporated. Now, add the butter, flax egg, and milk and pulse until everything is incorporated and coming together in a ball.

Remove the dough ball and, using a rolling pin, roll it out between two pieces of parchment paper until it is a little larger than your pie pan and ¼ to ½ inch thick. Press the dough into your pie pan. Because this dough is gluten-free, you don't have to worry about its getting overworked or tough by handling or pressing it into the pan. Make several holes with a fork all across the bottom of the dough, then bake according to the directions in your preferred pie recipe! This crust can be prepared in advance and frozen for up to 3 months, or refrigerated for up to 5 days, wrapped in parchment or plastic wrap and kept in a well-sealed container.

# ROSE & CHOCOLATE SILK PIE WITH MISO

### MAKES ONE 9-INCH PIE

French silk pie was the benchmark for all special occasions when I was growing up, a creamy chocolate pie in a buttery crust with a layer of whipped cream topping. This version is velvety chocolate with an umami touch of miso and roasted dandelion root. The leaves and flowers are made with rose and cocoa powder, mixed into leftover pie dough.

» **SIMPLE SWAPS** Purchase whipping cream (dairy-free or not) and premade piecrust to simplify the recipe. Feel free to leave out the dandelion root and miso. You can use arrowroot in place of the cornstarch.

**PIE**

2 recipes Go-To Gluten-Free Piecrust (page 156)

3 tablespoons unsweetened cocoa powder

One 13.5-ounce can full-fat coconut milk

1 cup milk of your choice

⅓ cup coconut sugar

1 tablespoon roasted dandelion root, powdered and sifted

1 teaspoon white miso paste

1 teaspoon pure vanilla extract

¼ cup organic cornstarch

1 teaspoon rose powder or cocoa powder or combination, for ½ to 1 cup prepared dough

Gluten-free all-purpose flour for dusting

**TOPPING**

Whipped cream (flavored with rose powder if desired)

2 to 3 ounces dairy-free semisweet chocolate (55 to 70%) of your choice, or a sprinkle of rose powder

Sprinkle of salt

Make the pie: Preheat your oven to 350°F. Prebake one recipe of the piecrust in a 9-inch pie pan for 10 to 15 minutes, then remove from the oven and let cool completely. In the meantime, begin making your pie filling.

Combine the cocoa powder, coconut milk and milk, coconut sugar, and dandelion root in a large saucepan over medium heat. Whisk until everything is well incorporated and then add the miso and vanilla. Transfer a few tablespoons of the liquid from the saucepan to a small bowl, add the cornstarch to the bowl, and whisk gently to form a roux. Once it becomes pourable, quickly whisk it into the saucepan mixture, continuing to heat over medium-low heat until thickened. Once thickened, use a spatula to scoop the chocolate filling into the baked piecrust, spreading it evenly and smoothing it out on top.

Chill the pie in the refrigerator for a few hours or overnight with a piece of parchment or plastic wrap on top.

Meanwhile, knead the rose and/or cocoa powder into the ½ to 1 cup of the remaining pie dough. The dough can be divided into two or three equal parts; rose rose can be added to one, cocoa powder to another, and the last can be left plain so there are variations in color for your flowers and leaves. Roll out the

*continued »*

dough on a GF-floured surface to about ½ inch thick. Use a 1½- to 2-inch round cookie cutter to cut out small disks of dough. If you have extra dough, you can cut out small leaf shapes to bake as well. Layer four disks at a time, overlapping each of them about halfway. Starting at one side, carefully roll the dough disks to form a flower. Holding the bottom of your flower, gently fold the edges of the circle back, flaring out the petals. Repeat until you've used all your dough.

Place your flowers on a baking sheet with any leaf cutouts and bake for about 10 minutes, until golden brown and cooked through.

Once the pie is completely cool, pipe on whipped cream topping and shave a little chocolate on top, using a grater, or add a sprinkle of rose powder. When your pie dough flowers have completely cooled, add them to the top of the whipped cream on the pie and serve.

# ROSE HIP CARAMEL APPLES

**YIELDS 6 TO 8 CARAMEL APPLES**

My daughter, Nila, inspired these caramel apples after requesting them during an apple harvest at our old farm in Española, New Mexico. There were nearly 50 old apple trees, so all fall and deep into winter, we ate our fill and then some. Caramel apples always epitomized fall for me—sweet caramel with a hint of salt wrapped around a green apple and covered in crunchy peanuts. This is a twist on the classic using honey, rose hips, and edible flowers.

8 small green apples, or 6 regular-size apples

1 cup honey or agave nectar

¾ cup full-fat canned coconut milk

2 tablespoons butter of your choice

¼ teaspoon salt

1 teaspoon pure vanilla extract

1 tablespoon powdered rose hips (optional)

Nettle seeds, peanuts (chopped finely), nuts or seeds of your choice, and dried edible flowers for topping

Wash and thoroughly dry your apples. Chill them in the refrigerator for about an hour before proceeding further. This isn't necessary, but might help the caramel stick better.

To make the caramel, you will want to gather all the ingredients together, as the process moves fast and requires your full attention. Additionally, have all the toppings prepared and ready to use wherever you are assembling the apples. Set a small to medium heatproof bowl near the stove and have ready six to eight food-safe sticks or short dowels to poke into the top of the apples, one for each apple; I use cottonwood branches.

Prepare the apples by removing the stems; just twist them until they come off. Push a stick through the core of each apple and set the apples on a parchment-lined baking sheet near your stove.

Begin making the caramel by heating a heavy-bottomed or nonstick skillet over medium heat. Pour in the honey and coconut milk. Use a whisk to mix them together, then continue to whisk. The mixture will often bubble up and foam, almost soapy in appearance; just keep on whisking and cooking over medium heat for 8 to 10 minutes.

*continued »*

You'll know the caramel is almost ready when the bubbles get much smaller and the top takes on a glossy and soft look. When you are whisking, the caramel will leave trails in the bottom of the pan before covering over again with the mixture. The caramel will also smell more like caramel and less like honey, and will grow darker in color. At this stage, add the butter, salt, and vanilla. Whisk until the butter is melted, then cook for 1 to 2 minutes longer.

Pour the caramel into your heatproof bowl and use a spatula to add the rose hip powder (if using), incorporating it fully. Now, roll an apple in the caramel and set it, on its base, on the parchment. The caramel should enrobe the apple, and if it doesn't or just slides off, you can add the caramel back to the pan and keep cooking for a few minutes. If the caramel is too thick, warm it slightly and add a teaspoon of coconut milk, whisking quickly, adding another teaspoon as needed to get the right consistency.

Sprinkle your preferred toppings onto the caramel as soon as it enrobes the apple. Repeat this with each apple until all are covered. As the caramel supply dwindles, you can use a spatula or butter knife to spread the caramel on the apples.

The apples can be eaten right away, or they will stay good for up to 3 days.

# ROASTED DANDELION ROOT "COFFEE"

**MAKES 6 TO 8 SERVINGS**

Fall is the time to harvest the powerfully medicinal dandelion root, roast it to a deep brown, and make a warm mug of this earthy, coffee-flavored drink. Dandelion is gathered after the first few frosts, when the energy of the plant moves underground and concentrates in the roots. The plant also undergoes chemical changes as the weather cools, such as inulin increasing and fructose decreasing. Inulin is a soluble, prebiotic fiber that helps balance blood sugar, support gut health, and much more. Roasted dandelion root powder is one of my favorite additions to fall and winter recipes, and I use it regularly throughout the book to enhance the nutrition, flavor, and medicine of meals.

❋ **FORAGER'S NOTE** Harvest the dandelion roots by using a small shovel or hori-hori to dig around the plant and carefully lift it out of the ground, to keep the roots whole.

2 to 5 dandelions, roots intact

Preheat the oven to 350°F. Wash the dandelions. Remove and reserve any smaller, thinner rootlets to dry for using in broths, soups, and teas. Chop the heartier roots into thin rounds. The leaves, stems, and flowers—if there are any left after the frost—can be made into Dandelion Vinegar (page 219) or composted.

Lay the rounds in a single layer across a dry baking sheet and bake for about 40 minutes, occasionally checking for doneness. The root should be fairly dark brown all the way through, and it will smell somewhat chocolaty.

Remove the dandelion roots from the oven and wait until they are cool to the touch. You can store the cool, completely dry roots in a sealed jar for up to a year, or make the rest of the recipe right away.

Powder the roasted dandelion roots as needed by placing the dried and roasted roots in an old coffee grinder or spice grinder, blending until they become a fine powder.

To make your coffee, add 1 teaspoon of the roasted dandelion roots to an 8-ounce cup of boiling water, steeping for 5 to 10 minutes and sweetening as desired.

# DANDELION ROOT DRINKING CHOCOLATE

**SERVES 1 OR 2**

This is a thick and delicious drinking chocolate; rich and slightly bitter roasted dandelion root adds depth and nutritional benefits, making this is a perfect fall drink. Dandelions and chocolate combine to create this energizing, warming beverage.

6 ounces water

3 ounces very dark (85 to 100%), good-quality chocolate of your choice, chopped roughly

1 teaspoon pure vanilla extract

1 to 2 tablespoons roasted dandelion root powder, finely ground

¼ teaspoon ground cinnamon, plus more for sprinkling

Pinch of cayenne pepper (optional)

Sweetener of your choice

Pinch of salt (optional)

Marigold petals

Bring the water to a simmer in a small saucepan over high heat and stir in the chocolate pieces. Turn off the heat.

Whisking quickly, add the vanilla, dandelion root powder, cinnamon, and pinch of cayenne (if using).

Add your sweetener of choice and a pinch of salt (if you're a salt lover like me). Pour into one or two cups.

Add marigold petals and a sprinkle of cinnamon on top to finish.

# RASPBERRY & ROSE HIP CORDIAL

MAKES 1 QUART-SIZE JAR

Cordials have a long history of use, rooted in the bustling apothecaries of Italy during the 15th and 16th centuries. Originally an alchemy of bitter and fragrant local herbs and wild-flowers, peels of citrus, and seeds of wild fennel, a cordial was a potion made for inspiring love and igniting libido, a curative dispensed for an illness that would not heal, or a preventative tonic to boost the immune system. From the Mediterranean, cordials made their way to England and other countries in Europe that preferred a more syrupy blend for mixing with alcohol or tonics.

In this recipe, I use raspberries and rose hips, both members of the prolific Rosaceae family that has been used for its heart-healing properties and myriad beneficial compounds. Raspberries are high in vitamins C and E, selenium, beta-carotene, lutein, and lycopene. This recipe can be made with other fruits or herbs, such as elderberry or fennel, and I make both alcoholic and nonalcoholic versions to have on hand for different needs and desires.

1½ cups crushed raspberries (from nearly 1 quart whole berries)

½ cup chopped and seeded fresh rose hips, or ¼ cup dried

3 or more cups brandy

1½ cups honey or sugar of your choice

Combine the berries and rose hips in a quart-size glass jar and pour in the brandy, covering the fruit completely. Allow the mixture to steep in the alcohol for 4 to 6 weeks, then strain into another jar through a sieve or fine-mesh strainer, pressing with a spoon to squeeze out as much of the fruit and floral juice as you can.

After straining through the sieve, strain back into your original jar through cheesecloth to be sure you remove any of the fine hairs from the rose hips. If you are using dried or seeded rose hips, the hairs likely will not be present and this step may not be necessary.

Pour the honey into the brandy-steeped raspberry mixture and stir well to combine. Save in a cool, dark space in your kitchen or refrigerate. Stir the mixture into tonic or sparkling water, add honey or sugar to your desired sweetness, and enjoy!

*continued »*

# NONALCOHOLIC RASPBERRY & ROSE HIP CORDIAL

**MAKES APPROXIMATELY 1 QUART**

1½ cups (nearly 1 quart) whole raspberries

1½ cups water

½ cup chopped and seeded fresh rose hips, or ¼ cup dried

3 to 5 tablespoons freshly squeezed lemon juice

2 cups honey or sugar

Combine the raspberries with 1 cup of the water in a medium saucepan and smash them a bit with the back of a spoon. Heat over medium-high heat. Once they come to a boil, add the rose hips. Simmer for 3 more minutes and remove from the heat and let steep, covered, for at least 2 hours or overnight.

Strain the juice into a jar through a sieve or fine-mesh strainer, pressing with a spoon to squeeze out as much of the fruit and floral juice as you can.

After straining through the sieve, strain into a quart-size glass jar through cheesecloth to be sure you remove any of the fine hairs from the rose hips. If you are using dried or seeded rose hips, the hairs likely will not be present and this step may not be necessary.

Heat the remaining ½ cup of water to a boil in a small saucepan, turn off the heat, and stir in the lemon juice and honey until dissolved. Stir the honey mixture into the raspberry mixture.

Label and add a lid to your jar of nonalcoholic cordial and store in the refrigerator for up to 3 weeks, or freeze for longer storage, thawing when ready to use. Add to sparkling water, stir into hot teas, or drizzle over desserts or treats.

# FALL DIGESTIVE BITTERS

**MAKES 1 QUART-SIZE JAR**

Digestive bitters are herbs, flowers, and some mushrooms, infused in alcohol, to be taken before or after meals, particularly helpful when eating heavier foods. They stimulate bitter receptors on the tongue, stomach, gallbladder, and pancreas, activating the digestive system to break down food and support the absorption of nutrients. Amaro is an Italian bitter liqueur that has become very popular in recent years, and it has been made for millennia by nonnas and monks in Italy. Every region is expressed in the myriad herbs of Amaro, often more than 20 at a time. Everywhere in the world, there are bitter foods and drinks taken for the benefit of digestion and gastronomical delight, and I encourage you to experiment with edible herbs and plants you love and/or that are regional.

» **SIMPLE SWAP** You can swap in vinegar for the vodka or brandy, which will change the flavor but will still work as a bitter.

Fresh peel of ½ grapefruit, lemon, or orange

¼ cup hawthorn berries

1 cinnamon stick

3 slices fresh ginger

1 tablespoon fennel seeds

1 teaspoon black peppercorns

2 tablespoons rose petals

¼ cup anise hyssop flowers or fresh fennel leaves

2 tablespoons fresh or dried calendula flowers

A few fresh or dried artichoke leaves

Vodka or brandy

Honey or other sweetener of your choice (optional)

Combine your fruits, spices, and herbs in a quart-size glass jar and cover with vodka or brandy. Label your jar and allow it to steep for 4 to 6 weeks. After this time, strain out the fruits, spices, and herbs, reserving the liquid. Take a dropperful or two 15 to 20 minutes before your meal, or enjoy in a glass of sparkling water, sweetened if you prefer.

# HAWTHORN BERRY BRANDY

**MAKES APPROXIMATELY 1 PINT-SIZE JAR**

Hawthorn berries are luminescent when ripe, red glowing beacons against fluttering dark green leaves. The color a hint of the remedy: hawthorn is a heart medicine. The berries, leaves, and flowers of the beloved hawthorn have been used to treat heart disease, strengthen the heart muscle and veins, and soothe irregular heartbeats. Hawthorn has also been used to support the whole body with anti-inflammatory and antioxidant properties. It has been used in both Traditional Chinese Medicine and other traditional herbal medicine practices across Europe and elsewhere in the world. When they emerge during the fall harvest, I love to make this elixir each year with hawthorn berries.

1 cup hawthorn berries, stems removed

1 cup brandy or vodka, or enough to cover the berries and fill the jar completely

Place the berries in a pint-size mason jar, filling about half the jar. Cover the berries completely with brandy or vodka. Put the lid on your jar and store in a cool, dark place for 6 to 8 weeks. At the end of these weeks, strain the liquid through a mesh sieve and store it at room temperature in a clean glass jar. Compost or discard the berries. You can sip this by the teaspoon, or enjoy it in sparkling water, drinks, and teas.

**NOTE** Do not eat the seeds of hawthorn berries, as they contain cyanogenic compounds, and always do your own research and due diligence. Every plant is different for everyone and there is no one-size-fits-all when it comes to herbs. Hawthorn berries in alcohol are safe; do not eat the seed and do not blend or crack open the seeds.

# WINTER

# CITRUS SALAD WITH FENNEL & CHICORY

**SERVES 4**

This winter salad is made with the colorful and bitter greens of chicory, balanced with the spice of radish, the crispness of fennel, the sour and sweetness of various citrus fruits, and the crunch of walnuts. This recipe is inspired by the after-dinner salads and digestive foods I remember from Sicily. A plate set out with tart, pithy slices of cedro, a variety of lemon, and sour orange would be paired with a small bowl of walnuts, both helping with digestion of fats and protein, and the uptake of nutrients. This salad is a welcome dose of sunshine in the long, cold months of winter.

» **SIMPLE SWAPS** If you do not have access to chicory, use arugula or any green of your choice, including radicchio or dandelion, which are in the same plant family. Use 1 tablespoon of freshly squeezed lemon juice and salt to taste in place of the preserved lemon. Use any combination of citrus fruits you like.

¾ cup walnuts

1 tablespoon honey

⅛ teaspoon Calabrian chile flakes, or a sprinkle of cayenne pepper (optional)

1 small sweet orange (Cara Cara or navel)

1 to 2 blood oranges

¼ grapefruit

1 tangerine

1 cup chicory leaves (radicchio or radicchio di Treviso)

7 to 10 slices radish (watermelon, daikon, or any radish of your choice)

½ fennel bulb, sliced thinly

⅛ to scant ¼ cup good olive oil

1½ tablespoons diced preserved lemon

Sea salt

Heat the walnuts in a small, dry skillet over low heat and pour in the honey. Sprinkle with a pinch of sea salt and add the chile flakes or cayenne, if you like spice. Stir quickly until the honey is absorbed into the walnuts. Turn off the heat once they absorb the honey and scoop them onto a small plate to cool. They will be caramelized, so once cool separate them for sprinkling over the salad.

Cut each of your fresh citrus fruits into rounds about ¼ inch thick, leaving the peel on the fruit. Once they are cut, slice off the peel from the outside. This will keep them intact as opposed to trying to cut them with the skin removed.

Arrange the salad in layers on a large plate, beginning with the chicory as the base layer, followed by the citrus, radish, and fennel.

Combine the olive oil and diced preserved lemon in a high-speed blender and blend. Pour the dressing on top of the salad, adding salt to taste and sprinkling the caramelized walnuts over the top to finish.

# ROASTED SQUASH & KALE SALAD WITH TAHINI & PRESERVED LEMON DRESSING

**SERVES 4 TO 6**

Roasted winter squash with creamy dressing and spiced, crispy chickpeas is a hearty and warming meal on a wintry day. This roasted salad finds its place on our holiday table, a balance of spice and color.

One 15-ounce can chickpeas, or about 1½ cups cooked chickpeas

3 tablespoons olive oil

¼ teaspoon harissa seasoning

¼ teaspoon turmeric powder

¼ teaspoon powdered thyme

¼ teaspoon garlic powder

1 winter squash (acorn, butternut, kabocha, delicata), halved and seeded, sliced in 1½-inch pieces

½ teaspoon yellow curry powder

Salt

2 bunches black kale, cut in ribbons (4 to 5 cups sliced)

2 teaspoons freshly squeezed lemon juice

1 grapefruit or blood orange, or ¼ cup pomegranate seeds

1 recipe Tahini & Preserved Lemon Dressing (recipe follows)

Sprinkle of edible flowers

Preheat the oven to 400°F. Drain the chickpeas and rinse them before placing in a small bowl. Stir 1 tablespoon of the olive oil into the chickpeas and add the harissa, turmeric, thyme, and garlic powder, stirring until the chickpeas are coated completely.

Transfer the chickpeas to a parchment-lined baking pan. Bake for 15 to 20 minutes, until crunchy and deep gold. Set aside.

Toss the squash in a large bowl with a tablespoon of the olive oil, plus the curry powder and a pinch of salt. Then, spread the squash onto the prepared pan used for the chickpeas. Bake the squash until soft in the center and crisp at the edges, 10 to 15 minutes. Remove the squash from the oven and set on a pan.

Place the ribboned kale in a medium bowl, and add 1 tablespoon of the olive oil, a sprinkling of sea salt, and the lemon juice. Toss to coat it completely, giving it a few squeezes with your hands to mix thoroughly. Spread the kale on the same prepared baking pan that was used for the squash and the chickpeas. Bake for 5 to 7 minutes.

Slice the grapefruit in rounds keeping the peel intact. Then cut the peel off the rounds, leaving the slices whole. Or skip the grapefruit and use ½ cup of pomegranate seeds. Layer the kale, squash, crispy chickpeas, and fruit on a large serving platter, and serve immediately with the preserved lemon tahini dressing drizzled over the top, sprinkled with edible flowers.

# TAHINI & PRESERVED LEMON DRESSING

**MAKES 1 CUP**

½ cup olive oil

¼ cup white hulled sesame seeds

¼ cup water

½ preserved lemon, about 1½ tablespoons (if you don't have preserved lemons, substitute the zest of ½ lemon, 3 tablespoons freshly squeezed lemon juice, and ¼ teaspoon salt)

Sea salt

1 garlic clove

Combine the olive oil, sesame seeds, and water in a high-speed blender and blend until smooth. Add the preserved lemon, salt to taste, and garlic and blend on high speed until creamy. Drizzle over the salad and save any leftovers for up to 2 weeks in the refrigerator.

# DREAMING MUSHROOM SIPPING BROTH

**SERVES 6 TO 8**

Broths are essential to the seasonal, culinary herbal kitchen, supporting what is needed, whether it is gut health, boosting the immune system, or a flavorful base for soups and stews. I created this mushroom-based broth to bring restful sleep and lucid dreams while staying rooted. Dreams have always been a fascination for me, a guiding force in my life. I often dream of plants before I meet them, or they will come in dreams to "tell" me to prepare them in a certain way. Vacillating between dreaming and insomnia for much of my life, I work with plants to support sleep and explore dreaming.

Mugwort and blue lotus flowers are the main dreaming herbs in this broth and have been used for relaxation, lucid dreaming, and divination for thousands of years. This is a broth made to sip in the evening before bed.

❈ **FORAGER'S NOTE** As with all plants, you must do your own due diligence when using new herbs, as everyone responds differently to every plant. Do not drink mugwort when pregnant.

*continued »*

5 cups assorted mushrooms
(shiitake, enoki, oyster, lion's
mane, porcini), dried or fresh

12 to 16 cups water

1 to 2 heads garlic

1 large red or yellow onion,
cut in half

4 carrots, chopped loosely

3 tablespoons burdock root, dried, or
1 fresh 6- to 8-inch root, chopped

3 to 4 kombu seaweed pieces, or
1 cup seaweed of your choice

2 slices citrus fruit of your choice,
or 1 tablespoon freshly
squeezed lemon juice

Leaves from 2 rosemary sprigs

One 3-inch knob fresh ginger,
chopped loosely

2 teaspoons sea salt, plus
more to taste

2 tablespoons mugwort

3 tablespoons miso
paste (optional)

2 to 3 tablespoons blue
lotus flower

Combine everything, except the blue lotus flower and salt, in a large pot over medium heat, cover with a heavy lid, and simmer for 2 hours. Turn off the heat, stir in the lotus flower, and cover again, letting the broth steep for 20 to 30 minutes.

Drain the vegetables from the broth and discard them, returning the broth to the pot over medium heat and stirring in the miso, if using, while the broth is hot but not boiling. Add salt to taste, at least 1 to 2 teaspoons, and enjoy this broth in the evening by ladling 4 to 6 ounces into a mug and sipping.

**NOTE** Use any mushrooms available to you, and substitute vegetables when needed. In fact, you can add any veggie scraps you have on hand! Try celery, onion skins, fennel, and carrots/tops. This always makes for a richer veggie broth with even more nutrition. Leave out mugwort or blue lotus if you do not have access to them.

# SMASHED COCONUT BEANS WITH GREENS

### SERVES 4 TO 6

This is a savory and simple meal for a weeknight. This meal comes together quickly and is a cozy bowl of comfort food. Serve with Winter Squash Rainbow Cornbread (page 147), over cooked grains, or with a crisp salad and roasted squash or potatoes.

1 tablespoon coconut oil or ghee

1 small onion, chopped

2 garlic cloves, chopped

1 tablespoon grated fresh ginger, or 1 teaspoon ginger powder

1 teaspoon turmeric powder

1 teaspoon yellow curry powder

2 cups cooked chickpeas

1¼ cup full-fat coconut milk

2 large tomatoes, chopped roughly, or one 13.5-ounce can diced tomatoes

2 cups chopped nettles, chard, kale, collards, or spinach

Sea salt and freshly ground black pepper

Sprinkle of cayenne pepper

¼ cup fresh cilantro, chopped

Heat the oil in a large skillet over medium heat and add the onion, stirring until it is translucent and becoming golden. Add the garlic and fresh ginger (if using) and sauté for a few minutes more, stirring frequently. Add the turmeric, powdered ginger (if using instead of fresh ginger), and curry powder, and then stir in the cooked beans, coconut milk, and chopped tomato.

Continue to simmer over low heat and, using a fork or the back of a large spoon, lightly mash about 30 percent of the beans in the skillet. Stir in the greens and cook until they soften and the tomato is melted. Add salt and pepper to taste and a sprinkle of cayenne. Top with fresh cilantro.

# HASSELBACK SWEET POTATO WITH HERBY WALNUT SAUCE

**SERVES 1 TO 2**

Hasselback potatoes are crispy on the outside and soft and buttery inside, with perfect slices that hold any sauce. The green sauce in this dish is a sumptuous mineral- and vitamin-rich delight, perfectly balancing the sweet density of the purple potato. Use foraged or grown greens in this recipe, powdered dry nettles, and a big handful of parsley or cilantro.

» **SIMPLE SWAPS** Replace the large purple sweet potato with a white sweet potato, two large russet potatoes, or four medium golden potatoes. Replace the walnuts with pumpkin seeds for a nut-free meal. Substitute 1 teaspoon of lemon zest and 1 tablespoon of freshly squeezed lemon juice for the preserved lemon, salting to taste.

## SWEET POTATO

1 large purple sweet potato

1 tablespoon olive oil

1 tablespoon butter of your choice

Sea salt and freshly ground
    black pepper

## HERBY WALNUT SAUCE

¼ cup olive oil

1 tablespoon preserved lemon

2 tablespoons walnuts

½ cup fresh parsley leaves or a
    combination of fresh wild
    greens, such as dandelion or
    blanched nettles

Lemon zest

2 tablespoons freshly squeezed
    lemon juice

1 teaspoon powdered nettles

Sea salt

¼ teaspoon sumac
    powder (optional)

Sprinkle of cayenne
    pepper (optional)

Make the sweet potato: Preheat the oven to 425°F. Place the sweet potato on your counter, parallel to the length of the counter. Place chopsticks or flat wooden spoons in front and behind the sweet potato to stop the knife from going all the way through when you cut. Thinly slice across the potato at a 90-degree angle to the chopsticks, stopping at the chopsticks to keep the base intact.

Heat the olive oil and butter, plus salt and pepper to taste in a small saucepan over medium heat, mixing well, until the butter is melted. Place the sweet potato in an oven-safe dish and brush it completely with the butter mixture, sprinkling with more salt as needed.

Bake the potato, uncovered, for 40 to 50 minutes, checking for doneness after 40 minutes. It should be crispy-skinned, but soft enough to eat on the inside.

Make the sauce: Combine the olive oil and preserved lemon in a food processor and blend well.

Add the walnuts, greens, lemon zest and juice, powdered nettles, salt to taste, sumac (if using) and cayenne (if using) and pulse lightly until the consistency is smooth but still textured.

Remove the potato from the oven and spoon the sauce on top while it is warm. Save any leftover sauce in a sealed container in the refrigerator or the freezer for later use.

# TRADITIONAL IRISH NETTLE & POTATO CAKES

**SERVES 4 TO 6**

When I travel, I love to connect with the food and the plants of the land, and in one of my ancestral homes of Ireland, I am always inspired by what I learn from plants there. These are a version of a traditional Irish potato cake that likely originated during famine times. Called arán bocht tí in Irish, which means something akin to "poorhouse bread," they were a staple food made simply with flour and mashed potatoes. I first had a version of these at an amazing restaurant called Aniar in Galway, and this recipe is based on its delicious potato cakes. Nettles are added to the batter, but feel free to leave them out or replace with 1 tablespoon of dried and powdered nettles. Eat these warm with butter and honey or a sprinkle of Forager's Everything Salt Blend (page 229).

2¾ cups gluten-free flour blend, plus more as needed

1 tablespoon baking powder

1 teaspoon salt

8 tablespoons (1 stick) cold butter or shortening of your choice

1⅓ cups cold cooked and mashed potato

1 tablespoon coconut milk or any milk

2 large eggs, beaten

1 cup fresh nettles, chopped finely or blended in a food processor

Handful of fresh herbs, such as rosemary or thyme, chopped

4 dropperfuls of concentrated chlorophyll, for bright green color (optional)

Preheat the oven to 350°F and line a baking sheet with parchment paper. Whisk together the gluten-free flour, baking powder, and salt in a medium bowl. Using a pastry cutter, knives, or a food processor, incorporate the butter until the blended mixture looks like wet sand. Mix the mashed potato into the blend until well incorporated. Stir in the milk, eggs, nettles, herbs, and chlorophyll (if using), until incorporated.

Form the dough into a ball, adding more flour as needed until the dough is soft but not overly sticky. Chill in the refrigerator for at least 20 minutes.

Remove from the refrigerator and roll out to about 1-inch thickness or enough to cut about ten 2½-inch-diameter rounds, using a circular cookie cutter or the lid of a mason jar. Transfer the dough rounds to your prepared baking sheet and bake for 15 minutes, or until a toothpick comes out clean when inserted in the center of a cake. Serve warm with butter and honey.

# CREAMY PORCINI PASTA

**SERVES 4**

This is a nourishing plate of comfort food, perfect for a quick and easy winter weeknight meal. The base is a creamy sauce with mushrooms and lemon zest, featuring the flavorful porcini mushroom. This recipe will work great with dry or store-bought mushrooms.

1 cup raw cashews

2 cups boiling water

12 ounces dried pasta

1 tablespoon olive oil or butter of your choice

1 garlic clove, chopped

1½ cups fresh mushrooms, chopped (cremini, porcini, oyster, or any you enjoy!)

½ teaspoon salt, plus more to taste

2 tablespoons nutritional yeast (optional)

2 tablespoons dried porcini mushrooms, ground

½ cup plain yogurt of your choice

Zest of 1 lemon (about ¼ teaspoon)

**VARIATIONS** Toppings to add that are delicious but not necessary: 1 tablespoon of toasted pine nuts, 2 to 4 tablespoons chopped fresh parsley or basil, sprinkle of red pepper flakes

Begin by soaking the cashews in boiling water for about 10 minutes.

Bring a pot of salted water to a boil and cook the pasta according to package instructions. Drain and set aside.

Heat the olive oil or butter in a large skillet over medium-low heat. Add the garlic and sauté for just a couple of minutes, until the scent releases. Now, add the mushrooms to the skillet and sauté for about 5 minutes, adding a generous sprinkle of salt and continuing to stir for a few more minutes.

Next, drain the soaked cashews and combine with the nutritional yeast (if using), salt, porcini mushroom powder, and yogurt in a blender. Blend on high speed until smooth. Add half of the cooked mushrooms to the blender and pulse a couple of times until just blended.

Add the blended mixture to the hot skillet that contains the remaining mushrooms and heat over medium-low heat for about 5 minutes, stirring quickly. The mixture will thicken rapidly. Stir the cooked pasta into the hot sauce and sprinkle the lemon zest on top to serve.

# GOLDEN DAL WITH HERBS & SPICES

**SERVES 4**

This is a warming and simple meal that is incredibly versatile and delicious. Dal (lentils) with tadka (fried spices in oil or ghee) is a traditional Indian food that is one of my favorite comfort meals. One of the ways I learned to cook was with my best childhood friend, David. Starting around age 9, we cooked together once a week for his forgiving parents. We would choose a recipe that sounded fun, walk to the store, buy the ingredients, and make it after school at his house.

After college, we both moved back to Chicago, started cooking together again, and invited friends to join us. We called it Wednesday Dinner, and it became a misfit supper club of 13 to 15 people from all walks of life, happily crammed into David's apartment in a neighborhood known as Little India. This recipe was on regular rotation during the Wednesday Dinner years, and I still make it almost once a week, adding foraged greens when I have them. I serve it over rice steamed with a spoonful of butterfly pea flowers and quick-pickled onions with rose hips.

4 cups vegetable broth or water

1 cup dried red lentils, rinsed

2 to 4 bay leaves

2 tablespoons nettle leaf, or ½ cup fresh nettles

1 tablespoon turmeric powder

½ teaspoon brown or black mustard seeds

¼ teaspoon fennel seeds

1 teaspoon cumin seeds

2 tablespoons ghee or coconut oil

1 to 3 garlic cloves, chopped

About ½ teaspoon sea salt, or to taste

Quick-Pickled Red Onion (page 236), fresh cilantro, and/ or edible flowers for garnish

Bring the broth or water to a boil in a large saucepan and stir in the rinsed red lentils and bay leaves. Let simmer until the lentils are nearly cooked, about 8 minutes.

Add the nettles and continue to simmer for the next 7 minutes, skimming away any of the scum that may have come to the surface, using a mesh sieve, then stirring in the turmeric powder. Turn off the heat.

Place the mustard seeds, fennel seeds, and cumin seeds in a small bowl. Then, heat the ghee in a small skillet over medium-high heat, add the garlic, and sauté for just a minute or two. Add the seed mixture to the pan and stir frequently so they don't burn. The mustard seeds will begin to pop in the pan. After 10 seconds or so, turn off the heat and pour the entire mixture into the dal, being careful not to burn yourself. Stir the spices into the dal, add salt to taste, and serve topped with quick-pickled onion, fresh cilantro, and/or edible flowers. Enjoy this with rice, flatbread, quinoa, baked sweet potato, or eat it on its own.

# YELLOW DOCK & NETTLE SEED CRACKERS

**MAKES 24 CRACKERS**

These are delicious and herby crackers made with nutrient-dense seeds, including yellow dock and nettle seeds that are high in healthy omega-3 fatty acids and energizing compounds. These crackers are perfect with savory or sweet toppings and quick pickles such as Quick-Pickled Red Onion with Rose Hips (page 236).

» **SIMPLE SWAPS** Add more sesame or chia seeds in place of nettle seeds and yellow dock seeds. Stir in 1 tablespoon of mushroom powder to increase the nutrition and umami flavor.

½ cup pumpkin seeds

2 tablespoons nettle seeds

2 tablespoons yellow dock seeds

1 cup ground flaxseeds

¼ cup chia seeds

⅓ cup sesame seeds

1 teaspoon sea salt

1 to 2 tablespoons finely chopped mixed fresh herbs (rosemary, thyme, and oregano), or 1 to 2 teaspoons dried

1 tablespoon mushroom powder (optional, for flavor)

1¼ cups water

**VARIATIONS** Try adding different herbs and spices: cumin, turmeric, garlic, curry, oregano, chili powder, seaweed, and so on.

Preheat the oven to 300°F. Blend or lightly pulse the pumpkin seeds in a blender to a small grind, but still a rough texture. Combine the pumpkin seeds and the rest of the seeds, salt, and herbs in a medium bowl. Add the mushroom powder (if using). Stir the water into the seed mixture until completely incorporated.

Divide the batter in half. On a flat surface, put down a baking sheet–size piece of parchment paper. Place another piece of parchment on top of the seed mixture, and roll out the dough to your desired thickness, ¼ to ½ inch thick.

Carefully slide a baking sheet under the bottom layer of parchment paper and remove the top layer of parchment. Smooth out any breaks with a spatula. Use a knife or pizza cutter to score the lines in the dough to mark 12 equal-size crackers. Repeat this entire process with the second half of the cracker dough on a second baking sheet. Bake for 1 hour, or until the crackers are golden brown across the top and getting crisp on the edges.

Remove from the oven and let cool completely before breaking the crackers along your scored lines.

# OAT, NETTLE & ROSE BANNOCKS

**SERVES 4 TO 6**

Food and plants have been the strongest threads I have in weaving my connection to my ancestors and these bannocks are especially significant in that sense. Bannocks are a delicious, unleavened oat bread from Scotland and Ireland, where many of my ancestors came from and where I am named for. Bannocks have been cooked over fires in the British Isles for hundreds of years, and were made to enjoy at celebrations or holidays such as Samhain and Imbolc, or St. Brigid's Day. They are sometimes given as offerings or eaten as a simple breakfast food with tea, similar to a scone. Oats have been used as a nervous system–soothing plant for the heart and digestion, and make for a hearty meal. I like to bake these as a celebratory food when winter begins to turn toward spring, adding the sweetness of honey, creamy butter and milk, a hint of roses, and energizing, green nettles and their seeds.

✳ **FORAGER'S NOTE** Before powdering dried nettle leaf in a coffee grinder or spice blender, remove the stems first.

» **SIMPLE SWAP** If you do not have nettles, replace them with more oat flour.

1½ cups sprouted or regular oats, plus 3 tablespoons for topping

1¼ cups oat flour, plus more for dusting

¾ teaspoon baking soda

1½ teaspoons Forager's Everything Salt Blend (page 229), or 2 to 3 teaspoons sea salt

1 tablespoon fresh rosemary or thyme leaves, diced finely, or 2 teaspoons dried

¼ cup powdered nettle leaf

1 tablespoon nettle seeds (optional)

2 tablespoons dried rose petals, plus 1 teaspoon for sprinkling on top

8 tablespoons butter of your choice, chopped, plus 2 tablespoons for the topping

¾ cup nearly boiled hot milk of your choice or boiled water

1½ tablespoons honey, plus 2 tablespoons for topping

2 to 3 dropperfuls of chlorophyll concentrate, to add a brighter green hue (optional)

Preheat the oven to 355°F and line a baking sheet with parchment paper. Combine the 1½ cups of oats, 1¼ cups of oat flour, baking soda, salt blend or salt, rosemary or thyme, and powdered nettle leaf in a food processor and pulse 30 times. The oats should be broken up at the end, but still textured.

Transfer the oat mixture to a large bowl and whisk in the 2 tablespoons of rose petals and the nettle seeds (if using). Add the chopped butter, then pour the hot milk or water on top, stirring quickly until the butter melts into the batter. Stir 1½ tablespoons of the honey into the batter.

Place a piece of parchment paper on a flat surface and dust generously with oat flour. Scoop the batter onto the parchment and flour as needed until you can spread it out, using your hands, to about 1½ inches thick. Use a cookie cutter to cut shapes, about 3 inches in diameter, from the dough and place them on the prepared baking sheet.

Bake for about 10 minutes. In the meantime, prepare a butter, honey, and oat topping. (This is optional but delicious.) Gently heat the remaining 2 tablespoons of butter in a small saucepan over medium heat and stir in the remaining 2 tablespoons of honey. Turn off the heat and stir in the remaining 3 tablespoons of oats. After the bannocks have baked for 10 minutes, remove the pan from the oven and spoon a small amount, about ½ teaspoon or so, of the honey mixture on each bannock, then place the pan in the oven for an additional 7 to 10 minutes, or until bannocks are beginning to get golden on top.

Remove from the oven and sprinkle with rose petals. Serve right away with tea.

# BUCKWHEAT & FORAGED SEED GRANOLA COOKIES

### MAKES 12 TO 14 COOKIES

These are lightly sweet and salty breakfast cookies loaded with energizing and nutrient-dense plants and whole grains. Buckwheat has a nutty and almost cinnamon flavor to it and is actually a gluten-free pseudocereal, high in protein and B vitamins, magnesium, copper, and manganese. It can help moderate blood sugar and is an essential staple in my kitchen.

» SIMPLE SWAPS  This recipe can be easily made with all buckwheat if you are allergic to oats. Substitute hemp or sesame for the nettle seeds. Substitute more buckwheat for the oats. Swap pumpkin seeds for the pecans if needing a nut-free recipe. Substitute demerara or brown sugar in place of the coconut sugar.

2 tablespoons blended flax or chia seeds plus ¼ cup water

1 cup unhulled buckwheat, soaked in water overnight, drained, and rinsed

1 cup rolled oats

⅔ cup pecan pieces, chopped

¼ cup nettle seeds

⅓ cup coconut sugar

½ cup pure maple syrup or applesauce

2 teaspoons ground cinnamon

¼ teaspoon salt

½ cup coconut oil, melted

Preheat the oven to 350°F and line a baking sheet with parchment paper or a silicone baking mat. Stir the blended seeds into the water, in a small bowl, and let sit as you prepare the rest of the recipe. Rinse the buckwheat thoroughly and then place in a large bowl. Add all the remaining ingredients, except the seed mixture, and stir well to incorporate fully. Now, add the seed mixture and stir to incorporate.

Spread the mixture evenly on your prepared baking sheet, using a spatula. Try not to leave too many holes. Use a round cookie cutter or mason jar lid to score cookie shapes in the wet mixture. This will make it easier to cut and separate the cookies after baking.

Bake for 10 to 15 minutes, then rotate the pan in the oven. Continue to bake for 10 to 15 more minutes and rotate again. Then, bake for 7 minutes and rotate, followed by 7 more minutes before removing the pan from the oven.

When you remove the cookies from the oven, place the cookie cutter over the scores you had made and cut through again while the cookies are warm. Let the cookies cool completely before removing from the pan.

You can eat these cookies on their own, saving the edge pieces for granola on top of yogurt of your choice. Or serve them as a perfect portable breakfast, or with the Butterfly Pea & Elderberry Poached Pears with Mascarpone-Style Rose Cream (page 203).

# ROSE ROLL-OUT COOKIES WITH CHOCOLATE & ROSE ICING

**MAKES 12 TO 14 COOKIES**

These cookies were a special request from my daughter, the love of my life, who inspires everything I do with her vision of beauty and magic. These are a take on a classic Chicago deli cookie: a little soft and chewy, with a melt-in-your-mouth icing on the top. These are filled with the heart-supportive medicine of rose, and glazed with glossy chocolate and rose icings.

## COOKIES

2½ cups blanched almond flour or hazelnut flour

¼ cup tapioca flour

¾ teaspoon sea salt

1½ tablespoons powdered rose petals

¾ teaspoon baking soda

2 teaspoons pure vanilla extract

½ cup melted coconut oil

2½ tablespoons beet juice (for color)

¼ cup pure maple syrup

Rose petals and rose finishing salt (see Wildflower Finishing Salts, page 226) to finish

## ROSE ICING

5 tablespoons maple butter

1 tablespoon rose powder

1 teaspoon beet juice

## CHOCOLATE ICING

6 tablespoons honey

½ cup 100% dark chocolate pieces, disks, or chopped chocolate of your choice

2½ tablespoons coconut cream (from the top of a can of full-fat coconut milk)

1 tablespoon pure vanilla extract

¼ teaspoon sea salt

Mix together the flours, salt, powdered rose petals, and baking soda in a large bowl. In a smaller bowl, stir together the vanilla, melted coconut oil, beet juice, and maple syrup. Stir the oil mixture into the flour mixture until well incorporated. Form a ball or tube of the dough, wrap it in parchment or wax paper, and chill in the refrigerator for at least 2 hours.

Preheat your oven to 350°F. Remove the dough from the refrigerator and have ready two parchment-lined cookie pans. Take two additional pieces of parchment paper about half the size of the baking pans and place the dough between them. Roll out the dough to about ½ inch thick and remove the upper parchment paper. Working quickly so the dough stays as cold as possible before going in the oven, use heart-shaped cookie cutters or a mason jar lid to cut out shapes. You should end up with about twelve 3-inch-wide cookies.

Place the cookie shapes on the prepared baking sheets; they won't spread much, so you can fit more on one baking sheet than usual. Bake for 10 to 12 minutes, removing them from the oven when they are becoming golden underneath and lightly golden on top. Let them cool completely on the pans and prepare the icings as they cool.

Make the rose icing: Mix together all the rose icing ingredients in a small bowl until the icing is smooth with no lumps.

**NOTE** You can save the chocolate icing from this recipe by storing it in the refrigerator for up to 3 months and melting it to use as a topping for ice cream and other treats.

Make the chocolate icing: Heat the honey in a large skillet over low heat, stirring frequently. When the honey becomes hot, add the chocolate and turn off the heat, whisking rapidly to incorporate the chocolate. Once the chocolate is melted completely, stir in the coconut cream, vanilla, and salt, then transfer to a small bowl. Let the icing cool slightly before applying to the cookies. Keep in mind that it will continue to harden as it cools.

When the cookies are completely cooled, use a knife or spoon to apply the icings, alternating between chocolate or rose iced cookies, or making designs with the icings as you wish. While the icings are still a bit wet, top the cookies with rose petals and rose finishing salt, and allow the icings to cool and solidify before enjoying.

# NETTLE MACARONS WITH SPRUCE OR ROSE BUTTERCREAM

**MAKES APPROXIMATELY 36 MACARONS**

Macarons are a favorite classic French dessert—with Italian roots!—made traditionally with almond flour and egg white. The Parisian version, which we have all come to know as the little sandwiches filled with ganache, jelly, or buttercream, became popular in the 20th century and inspired this recipe.

These macarons incorporate some favorite foraged and seasonal ingredients, and use maple sugar in place of powdered and granulated sugar. The flavor of nettle and spruce buttercream are a perfect, delicate blend in macarons.

» SIMPLE SWAPS You can substitute 1½ tablespoons dried and powdered rose petals for the spruce in this recipe. Use superfine sugar in place of the maple sugar.

## MACARON COOKIES
Egg whites from 3 eggs (100 g)

1¼ cups plus 2 tablespoons (130 g) almond flour

4 teaspoons (10 g) powdered and sifted nettle leaf

¾ cup plus 1 tablespoon (120 g) powdered maple sugar or confectioners' sugar

¼ teaspoon cream of tartar

1 dropperful of green liquid chlorophyll or green food dye or gel

¼ cup (90 g) granulated maple sugar

Make the macarons: One to three nights before making the macarons, place the egg whites in the refrigerator, in a covered bowl, with holes in the covering or the lid partially open, to "age" them, then warm the egg whites to room temperature the day of cooking.

Line two baking sheets with parchment. Sift the almond flour, nettle powder, and powdered sugar into a bowl, then transfer this mixture to a food processor and pulse quickly about 20 times; be sure to only just pulse, not process continuously, or the mixture will get oily and consequently will collapse the egg whites. Sift the mixture back into its bowl; this may seem tedious, but it's so helpful for the end result.

Whip the egg whites with an electric mixer until they get frothy, and then add the cream of tartar and coloring, continuing to mix until the egg whites begin to form soft peaks; then very slowly add the granulated maple sugar as you continue to beat. If added too quickly, the weight of the sugar will collapse the protein in the eggs. Beat until there are really stiff peaks.

*continued »*

## SPRUCE BUTTERCREAM

½ cup (1 stick) butter of your choice (I use a vegan brand, Miyokos), at room temperature

1 cup blended and powdered coconut or maple sugar, or confectioner's sugar

1 tablespoon dried and finely ground fir or spruce needles

1 teaspoon pure vanilla extract

Salt

**NOTES** Macarons can be finicky, so this recipe will be best if ingredients are measured with a kitchen scale. All your ingredients should be at room temperature. Use a coffee grinder or spice grinder to "powder" your sugar if you are using maple sugar. Using a printable macaron template under parchment or a silicone mat with macaron templates can make piping much easier. Make sure everything you use is very dry and clean.

Once the peaks are stiff, use a spatula to slowly fold one-third of the almond flour mixture into the egg whites, making figure eights in the batter as you go along. Slowly continue to add one-third of the almond flour mixture at a time, folding gently until the batter looks like molten lava and forms and holds the figure eight in the bowl.

Transfer the mixture to a piping bag and pipe your macarons into 1-inch disks on your prepared baking sheets. Pick up the baking sheets and carefully slam them down on your work surface 6 to 10 times, knocking any air bubbles out of the macarons. Let the macarons sit on their pans on the counter for at least 1 hour. The tops must be dry, forming a thin skin, before baking, or the characteristic "feet" on the bottom of the cookies will not form.

Preheat the oven to 300°F and bake the macaron cookies for 13 to 15 minutes, rotating at the halfway point, then remove from the oven and let them cool completely before filling.

While the cookies cool, make your buttercream: Cream the butter, using a mixer, and slowly add the sugar, beating until it is incorporated. Scrape down the sides of the bowl with a spatula and continue to beat until the mixture is smooth. Continuing to cream, add the powdered spruce needles and vanilla extract. Whip until completely smooth, then transfer to a piping bag.

To fill the macarons, pipe a small disk of buttercream onto the center of one overturned macaron cookie and gently place another macaron cookie on top to sandwich it all together. Repeat until all your macarons are filled.

# DANDELION ROOT MACARONS WITH BLOOD ORANGE & CHOCOLATE BUTTERCREAM

MAKES APPROXIMATELY 36 MACARONS

This second variation of the beloved macaron incorporates the rich, coffeelike flavors of roasted dandelion root with chocolate and blood orange. Please see the notes in the Nettle Macarons recipe (page 199) for more tips and tricks to get the most delicious end result.

## MACARON COOKIES
Egg whites from 3 eggs (100 g)

1¼ cups plus 2 tablespoons (130 g) almond flour

4 teaspoons (10 g) roasted dandelion root, powdered

⅛ teaspoon ground cinnamon

¾ cup plus 1 tablespoon (120 g) powdered maple sugar or confectioners' sugar

¼ teaspoon cream of tartar

¼ cup (90 g) granulated maple sugar

## BLOOD ORANGE & CHOCOLATE BUTTERCREAM
½ cup butter of your choice, at room temperature

¾ cup coconut sugar, blended and powdered, or any powdered sugar

¼ cup unsweetened cocoa powder

Zest of 1 blood orange or 1 small navel orange

1 teaspoon pure vanilla extract

Salt

Make the macarons: One to three nights before making the macarons, place the egg whites in the refrigerator, in a covered bowl, with holes in the covering or the lid partially open, to "age" them, then warming the egg whites to room temperature the day of cooking.

Line two baking sheets with parchment. Sift the almond flour, dandelion root powder, cinnamon, and powdered sugar into a bowl. Transfer this mixture to a food processor and pulse quickly about 20 times. Be sure to only just pulse, not process continuously, or the mixture will get oily and consequently will collapse the egg whites. Sift the mixture back into its bowl; this may seem tedious, but it's so helpful for the end result.

Whip the egg whites with an electric mixer until they get frothy, and then add the cream of tartar, continuing to mix until the egg whites begin to form soft peaks; then very slowly add the granulated maple sugar as you continue to beat. If added too quickly, the weight of the sugar will collapse the protein in the eggs. Beat until there are really stiff peaks.

Once the peaks are stiff, use a spatula to slowly fold one-third of the almond flour mixture into the egg whites, making figure eights in the batter as you go along. Slowly continue to add one-third of the almond flour mixture at a time, folding gently until the batter looks like molten lava and forms and holds the figure eight in the bowl.

*continued »*

Transfer the mixture to a piping bag and pipe your macarons into 1-inch disks on your prepared baking sheets. Pick up the baking sheets and carefully slam them down on your work surface 6 to 10 times, knocking any air bubbles out of the macarons. Let the macarons sit in their pans on the counter for at least 1 hour. The tops must be dry, forming a thin skin, before baking, or the characteristic "feet" on the bottom of the cookies will not form.

Preheat the oven to 300°F and bake the macaron cookies for 13 to 15 minutes, rotating at the halfway point, then remove from the oven and let them cool completely before filling.

While the cookies cool, make your buttercream: Cream the butter, using a mixer and slowly add the sugar, beating until it is incorporated. Scrape down the sides of the bowl with a spatula and continue to beat until the mixture is smooth. Continuing to cream, add the cocoa powder, blood orange rind, vanilla, and salt. Whip until completely smooth, then transfer to a piping bag.

To fill the macarons, pipe a small disk of buttercream onto the center of one overturned macaron cookie and gently place another macaron cookie on top to sandwich it all together. Repeat until all your macarons are filled.

# BUTTERFLY PEA & ELDERBERRY POACHED PEARS WITH MASCARPONE-STYLE ROSE CREAM

**SERVES 3 TO 4**

These sparkling deep-purple pears make a light and elegant dessert or breakfast, with the fruit poached to the color of gemstones, served with a generous spoonful of the creamy and slightly tart mascarpone. My daughter and I made this often at the start of the pandemic to cheer ourselves up, eating it for breakfast with Buckwheat & Foraged Seed Granola Cookies (page 194). It calls for Nettle "Champagne" (page 84) as the base, but any dry, hard cider or nonalcoholic sparkling water will work just as well.

2 cups sparkling hard cider or Nettle "Champagne" (page 84)

2 tablespoons honey or sweetener of your choice

½ cup water

½ split vanilla bean, or 2 teaspoons pure vanilla extract

¼ cup butterfly pea flowers, dried

2 tablespoons elderberries or blueberries

1 cinnamon stick

4 crushed cardamom pods

Squeeze of lemon juice

3 to 4 Bosc pears, slightly firm, not ripe

1 recipe Mascarpone-Style Rose Cream (recipe follows), or whipped coconut cream

Prepare the liquid that the pears will be cooked in by selecting a small to medium saucepan that will fit the pears snugly and allow them to be submerged under the liquid. Combine all the ingredients, except the pears and rose cream, in the pan and begin to warm over medium heat.

Peel the whole pears with a vegetable peeler and try not to remove the stem. Add the peeled pears to the liquid right away, laying them on their sides so they are submerged in the liquid. Cook them for 20 to 25 minutes.

Remove the pears from the sauce and place them in individual bowls. Return the saucepan with the sauce to the heat and simmer until the liquid is reduced to about one-third of what it was originally. Pour some of the reduced sauce over each pear.

Serve with the Buckwheat & Foraged Seed Granola Cookies for a special breakfast or brunch, or as an elegant dessert with the Mascarpone-Style Rose Cream or whipped coconut cream.

*continued »*

# MASCARPONE-STYLE ROSE CREAM

**MAKES 4 TO 6 SERVINGS**

1 cup raw cashew pieces

⅓ cup plain whole yogurt of your choice

2 tablespoons plus 1 teaspoon freshly squeezed lemon juice

1 teaspoon rose powder

1 teaspoon pure maple syrup

Sprinkle of sea salt or rose finishing salt (see Wildflower Finishing Salts, page 226)

Bring a small pot of water to a boil and place the cashews in a bowl. Once the water is boiling, pour it over the cashews so they are submerged, then let them sit for 20 minutes. Drain the cashews, combine them with all the remaining ingredients in a high-speed blender, and blend until silky smooth.

**VARIATION**  Leave out the rose powder and substitute unsweetened cocoa powder plus ¼ teaspoon of ground cinnamon, or leave it plain.

# SUGAR-ON-SNOW

SERVES 6 TO 8

Sugar-on-snow is a longstanding tradition in my family; maple syrup is heated and poured over fresh snow, served with a side plate of crunchy dill pickles (see photo on page 172). It goes all the way back to when my grandmother Jeanette grew up helping out on her grandmother's maple sugar farm in Vermont, in the early 1900s. She passed on this tradition to us by saving snow in the freezer for our annual picnics in summer. She'd lay out baking sheets of snow on the checkered tablecloth and pour hot maple syrup over the top, so we could twirl our forks in it, caramelized maple sugar gathered up in sweet strands. This delicious treat can be enjoyed in summer or winter, and we do a little of both in our family.

Enough clean, fresh snow to cover a baking sheet

½ to 1 cup real maple syrup

1 tablespoon butter of your choice (not necessary, but some people prefer this addition)

**NOTE** This recipe will not work if you don't use real maple syrup, so make sure you are sourcing correctly, or even tap your own if you can! Please do your own tree due diligence on whether snow is okay for you to eat.

Collect enough clean, fresh snow to fill a baking sheet about ½ inch or so deep all the way across. Leave the snow outside in the cold, or in a freezer if the weather is warming outside, and bring it in when you're ready to make the syrup.

Place the maple syrup in a large saucepan and start heating it over medium heat. Attach a candy thermometer to the side of the pot so that it's in the syrup but not touching the sides or bottom of the pot. Bring the syrup to around 235°F on the candy thermometer. The top of the syrup will look smooth and soft, after being frothy and bubbly for several minutes.

If adding butter, now is the time. Turn off the heat and stir in the butter quickly. Remove the syrup from the stove and pour it in thin ribbons across the snow. Twirl the syrup immediately with forks or ice pop sticks, as it hardens extremely fast. Eat fresh, or, if you want to save maple sugar pops, twirl each on an ice pop stick and freeze to eat later.

# CHOCOLATE-DIPPED BLOOD ORANGES WITH FORAGED & FLOWER TOPPINGS

**MAKES 2 CUPS**

These are a beautiful a treat, a perfect holiday gift, or addition to a winter table. Blood oranges are prized in Sicily, likely introduced a few thousand years ago. They were reserved for royalty and are enjoyed for their brilliant color and sweet-tart flavor. Blood oranges are rich in anthocyanin, which gives them their characteristic hue and may have heart-healing, inflammation-reducing benefits. The skin of the blood orange is both an excellent digestive and has a lovely but strongly bitter taste. If you prefer a less bitter treat, a swipe of honey or sugar and/or removing the orange peel will make this recipe sweeter.

» **SIMPLE SWAPS** Sprinkle with ground cinnamon and a finishing salt if you do not have any flowers or nettle seeds. You can use any citrus you like or have available, but blood oranges are ideal for this recipe.

---

2 or more blood oranges, or citrus of your choice

1 tablespoon honey (optional)

One to two 3.5-ounce 72% dark chocolate bars of your choice

Assorted dried edible flowers, such as rose petals or calendula

Sprinkle of salt to finish

Slice the oranges thinly into rounds. The rind is edible and really good for you but is bitter, so just trim it off carefully after slicing the oranges into rounds, if you wish.

If you prefer a sweeter orange, brush each slice with honey and place in a dehydrator to dry them. Alternatively, if you don't have a dehydrator, set your oven on the lowest possible setting and place the orange slices on top of a cooling rack. Place the cooling rack on top of a baking sheet and place this in the oven, leaving the oven door open a crack so the oranges don't become too hot. Check your oranges after 30 minutes; I love mine just slightly juicy in the center, but the drier they are, the longer they will keep. Bake them until they reach your desired texture and then set them aside.

Heat the chocolate in a double boiler until melted. You can make your own double boiler by placing a heatproof bowl on top of a small saucepan filled halfway with water. The water shouldn't touch the bowl.

Line a baking sheet with parchment paper and have it at the ready. Gather your edible flowers and salt and place these beside the pan.

Once the chocolate is melted, dip the oranges halfway and lay them on the parchment paper. Quickly add your flowers and just a sprinkle of salt. Let the chocolate cool and harden on the oranges and then assemble on a plate to enjoy. The chocolate-covered oranges will keep for 2 weeks or longer in a sealed container in the refrigerator.

# CHOCOLATE
# FLOWERING MENDIANTS

**MAKES 10 TO 12 SERVINGS**

When I became a chocolatier many years ago in New Mexico, mendiants were one of the first things I learned to make, tempering the chocolate by hand. Mendiants originated in Provence, France, as part of 13 desserts traditionally made for holidays; and are chocolate disks with nuts and fruits nestled in the center. Mendiant means "beggars' alms" and was made to be an austere offering that represented an order of monks of a similar name. I think of these as a bite-size love spell calling the flowers and plants back to bloom. You can add anything you have on hand, from nuts to seeds, spruce or fir, to any dried edible flowers and herbs, such as lavender or rosemary. You can even sprinkle a pinch of Wildflower Finishing Salts (page 226) on top.

6 to 10 ounces 72% dark chocolate of your choice, chopped

⅛ cup toppings (edible flowers, conifers, chopped nuts, seeds, herbs, finishing salts, etc.)

Wildflower Finishing Salts (page 226), for decorating (optional)

Make sure all kitchen tools that come in contact with the chocolate are completely dry, as any water droplets will cause the chocolate to "seize" and it will not temper. You will need a candy or cooking thermometer for this recipe. Have that ready off to the side of your stove. On another workspace, prepare a parchment-lined baking sheet and ready your toppings.

Start by placing a medium, heatproof bowl on top of a saucepan that is filled about one-third with water; the water shouldn't touch the bowl while it is simmering or it can scorch the chocolate. You can also use a standard double-boiler if you have one. Turn the heat beneath the saucepan or double boiler base to medium-high heat.

Place about two-thirds of the chocolate in the bowl or top of your double boiler and melt, stirring frequently and measuring the temperature until the thermometer registers around 115°F. Remove the bowl/top from the double boiler.

Now, you will add your "seed" chocolate, which is the remaining one-third of the chocolate. Vigorously stir in the unmelted chocolate until the temperature drops to 84°F. This can take a while—sometimes up to 10 to 15 minutes, but it will happen!

You can speed up the process by setting the bowl of heated chocolate in an ice bath as you stir, making sure not to get water in the chocolate.

Finally, place your bowl back on the saucepan or double boiler base, again over medium-low heat, for 5 to 10 seconds at a time, until the chocolate temperature reaches 89°F. Remove from the heat as soon as it reaches 89°F. Now the chocolate is tempered properly. It can be tempered over and over again by bringing it back to 89°F, using more "seed" chocolate, a little time on the double boiler, or microwaving for 5 to 10 seconds at a time.

Using a small spoon, scoop about 1 teaspoon of tempered chocolate onto the prepared baking sheet in the form of a disk. Continue to do this until you have filled the baking sheet with small disks. Have your toppings ready and sprinkle a little in the center of each chocolate disk. Allow them to set, then serve, or store them at room temperature where they will remain stable.

WINTER

# MEYER LEMON BUNDT CAKE WITH ROSE, BLOOD ORANGE & SUMAC ICING

**SERVES 8**

Citrus season is the highlight of winter for me; in the midst of long cold nights, there is sunshine coming through in Meyer lemons, grapefruits, and blood oranges. This time of year leaves very little to forage in the colder parts of the world, so I always save some of my foraged sumac to process in winter. Sumac adds a tangy burst to all it touches, including the drizzle icing for this cake. This is a dense cake and will not rise significantly, filling the Bundt pan about halfway up. It is stout but hearty, perfect for winter breakfast, brunch, or dessert.

» **SIMPLE SWAP** Sumac is a delicious tree or shrub that grows wild in many places, and it can often be found in the spice section of a store, or can be replaced with 1 teaspoon or more orange zest.

## CAKE

Coconut oil or butter of your choice for pan

Oat flour for pan

2 tablespoons ground flaxseeds plus ¼ cup water

1 cup oat flour

1 cup sorghum flour

1 cup blanched almond flour

1 teaspoon baking soda

½ teaspoon sea salt

1 cup plain yogurt of your choice

½ cup pure maple syrup

Zest and juice of ½ Meyer or regular lemon

2 teaspoons pure vanilla extract

¼ cup dried calendula petals (optional)

Sumac, blood orange, and rose icing

¼ cup coconut butter

2 tablespoons honey or sweetener of your choice

1 to 2 tablespoons beet juice or red food coloring of your choice

1 teaspoon sumac, plus more for sprinkling

1 tablespoon blood orange juice or lemon juice

Grated rind of ½ blood orange or small navel orange

2 tablespoons coconut cream (from the top of a can of full-fat coconut milk), plus more as needed

## TOPPINGS

1 teaspoon calendula petals

½ teaspoon rose petal powder and rose petals

Finishing salt, such as Wildflower Finishing Salts (page 226)

Sumac powder

Make the cake: Preheat the oven to 350°F. Oil or butter and flour a 10-cup Bundt pan (the batter will not fill the pan to the top) and dust with oat flour.

Stir together the water and flaxseeds in a small bowl and let sit for 5 minutes. Whisk together the flours, calendula petals, baking soda, and sea salt in a medium bowl. Then, in a stand mixer fitted with the attachment or using a hand mixer and a separate medium bowl, combine the yogurt, maple syrup, lemon zest and juice, and vanilla. Pour the yogurt mixture into the flour mixture and mix until everything is incorporated.

Pour the batter into your prepared Bundt pan and bake for 25 to 35 minutes, until the center is fully baked. Remove the cake from the oven and allow it to cool completely before icing.

Make the icing: Combine all the icing ingredients in a small bowl, whisking or blending until completely smooth. If the coconut butter is hard, warm it gently in a small pan over low heat or for 5 to 10 seconds at a time in a microwave-safe bowl in a microwave. Taste the icing before adding it to the cake, adding more sweetener as desired.

Pour the icing over the cooled cake and sprinkle with calendula petals, rose powder and petals, finishing salt, and sumac powder.

# FOREST WASSAIL

**SERVES 8 TO 10**

Wassail is a warming, spiced apple cider drink, an ancient brew made to honor the orchard that fed us the previous year, with the hope it will continue to fruit in the coming year. Wassailing is a centuries-old ritual, a community gathering and offering to the land, singing songs of gratitude, welcoming a new year and season of growth, and asking for protection for the plants and trees.

Wassail has pre-Christian roots that stretch across the British Isles and beyond. In the Norse tradition, wassail would have been called *ves heil*, and in English, *was hál*, both meaning something close to "good health" or "good fortune." It is a perfect hot drink to celebrate the season, and I love to add fresh spruce and roasted apples to celebrate the plants where I live, offering generous pours back to the trees.

» SIMPLE SWAP  Any edible conifer needles can be swapped for spruce, or just leave it out and celebrate the apple harvest.

3 apples

½ teaspoon ground cinnamon, plus a sprinkle for the apples

8 cups nonalcoholic, unpasteurized apple cider or apple juice

3 cinnamon sticks, plus more for serving

¼ teaspoon ground cloves

Sprinkle of ground nutmeg

3 tablespoons dried hawthorn berries

2 tablespoons elderberries

1 tablespoon rose hips

1 to 3 tablespoons spruce, fir, or pine needles

1 tablespoon freshly squeezed grapefruit or lemon juice

¼ cup cranberries

1 cup Hawthorn Berry Brandy (page 171) or regular brandy (optional)

Preheat the oven to 350°F and line a baking sheet with parchment paper. Slice the apples horizontally into rounds, removing the pits, and arrange the rounds in a single layer on the prepared baking sheet. Sprinkle with cinnamon and bake for 10 to 15 minutes, until soft.

When the apples are done baking, transfer them to a large, heavy-bottomed saucepan. Add all the remaining ingredients, except the brandy (if using), to the pot and bring to a gentle simmer over low heat. Stir in your dreams and intentions for the New Year, thanking the plants that went into your brew. Cover and continue to simmer over low heat for 20 minutes to an hour, then turn off the heat.

Alternatively, if you have a slow cooker, combine all the ingredients, except the brandy (if using), in the cooker, cover, and cook on LOW for about 4 hours.

Strain the fruits and spices out of the wassail, reserving the liquid, then stir in the brandy while the wassail is still warm. Pour the wassail back into its saucepan or slow cooker to keep it warm. Ladle into mugs and serve with a cinnamon stick.

# HAWTHORN & ROSE DRINKING CHOCOLATE

**SERVES 4 TO 6**

This is a thick and creamy drinking chocolate, a departure from an American-style hot chocolate. It is meant to be imbibed in smaller quantities, filled with the medicinal magic of rose hips, rose petals, and hawthorn berries. Hawthorn and rose have been used as heart medicines, both in the Rosaceae family, known for their ability to soothe the heart both on physical and emotional levels. This drinking chocolate is a cup of heart-loving, immune-boosting comfort, with warming cinnamon and a dose of vitamin C from the rose hips.

¼ cup seeded rose hips

4 cups water

¼ cup dried hawthorn berries

1 cinnamon stick

1 or 2 slices fresh ginger, or
   2 teaspoons ginger powder

2 tablespoons rose petals

Zest and juice of 1 blood orange

10 to 12 ounces 80 to 90% dark
   chocolate of your choice

2½ tablespoons honey, plus
   more to taste

2 teaspoons pure vanilla extract

¾ teaspoon sea salt or rose
   finishing salt (see Wildflower
   Finishing Salts, page 226)

2 teaspoons ground Ceylon
   cinnamon, ¼ teaspoon
   reserved for sprinkling on top

Blend 2 tablespoons of the rose hips in a spice grinder or coffee grinder until they are a fine powder. Combine the water, hawthorn berries, cinnamon stick, 2 tablespoons of the seeded and whole rose hips, and ginger slices (if using) in a large saucepan and bring to just a boil over medium heat.

Lower the heat to a simmer and add the rose petals (reserving ¼ teaspoon to use for topping) and orange zest and juice.

Turn off the heat and cover; let steep for at least 30 minutes.

Strain the mixture through a mesh sieve; squeeze out the liquid from the solids and discard them. Now, pour the liquid back into the saucepan and place over low heat.

Chop the chocolate roughly and stir into the mixture on the stove, a little at a time, until it is all just melted into the liquid. Do not let the chocolate boil or get too hot—it burns quickly and easily. Turn off the heat as soon as the chocolate begins to melt and continue to whisk until it is melted completely into the liquid.

Whisk in the powdered rose hips, honey, vanilla, salt and ground cinnamon, and ground ginger (if using). Taste and add more ground ginger, salt, honey, or cinnamon as needed.

Pour into cups and sprinkle the powdered rose hips, reserved rose petals, and cinnamon on top.

# HOMEMADE PANTRY THROUGH THE SEASONS

# DANDELION FLOWER SYRUP

**MAKES APPROXIMATELY 3 CUPS**

Dandelion flower syrup is a dreamy golden treat made with the shining first blooms of spring. Spring is a time when the plants are pushing all their energy into their blossoms, making it the optimal harvest for the medicinal qualities and the bright flavors of wild ingredients. Dandelion syrup can be used right away or frozen for use in granitas, snow cones, or warm drinks in winter. Enjoy it poured over pancakes or waffles, in sparkling cocktails, or added to ice pops.

❋ **FORAGER'S NOTE** Harvest the dandelion blooms, making sure you have identified them correctly, and always leave a large amount for the pollinators. Keep the green bottoms on the dandelion, as this part contains many of the medicinal qualities.

2 cups water

1 cup dandelion blooms

Honey or sugar in equal quantity to the strained dandelion liquid

Bring the water to a simmer over medium heat, add the blooms, turn off the heat, and cover for 1 to 2 hours to let the dandelions steep. Strain into a small saucepan, squeezing the blooms against a mesh sieve or in a mesh bag, then discard the solids. Reheat the dandelion infusion to a near boil, then turn off the heat. Stir in the honey or sweetener of your choice, bottle, and label. This can be frozen for later use.

# DANDELION VINEGAR

**MAKES 1 PINT-SIZE JAR**

Dandelions are a harbinger of spring, providing a wave of yellow blooms that go on for weeks or even months all across the world. The humble dandelion is a symbol of joy and resilience and is a wonderful addition to the spring medicine cabinet. Dandelions are a bitter herb, helping to aid digestion; the inulin-rich roots of the dandelion set the stage for healthy gut flora to proliferate.

Dandelions are nutrient dense, adding a large dose of minerals and vitamins, including potassium, vitamins A, C, and D, and B vitamins. Dandelions may help to clear the blood and lymph of toxins, support liver and skin health, and assist with the reduction of high cholesterol and blood pressure. Cider vinegar extractions can be great for pulling the minerals out of a plant, and I add a teaspoon of this vinegar to my water as a daily supplement.

2 to 3 dandelion plants, including roots, stems, leaves, and some flowers

Enough cider vinegar to cover the plants in a pint-size jar

Soak your dandelions in a bowl of cold water, rinsing any dirt from the roots and leaves.

Finely chop, including the stems and leaves. Place the dandelions in a clean pint-size glass jar, filling the jar at least halfway with them. Pour cider vinegar all the way to the top of the jar and use a knife to stir it all together, making sure everything is well covered in vinegar.

Cover the mouth of the jar with a square of parchment paper and screw the lid on over the paper. Label your jar, adding the date, where you harvested, and any love notes. Give it a little shake and leave in a dark space for at least 1 week, and up to 2 months.

Strain out the dandelion plant material, reserving the vinegar and pouring it back into your jar. This vinegar can be used in the Dandelion Switchel recipe (page 83). Alternatively, you could add this vinegar to dressings, sauces, sparkling water, or soups.

# REDBUD FLOWER "CAPERS"

**MAKES APPROXIMATELY 1 CUP**

This is a flavorful and delicious way to enjoy the citrus burst of redbud flowers. The redbud tree produces one of my favorite edible flowers, illuminating spring with its magenta inflorescence. Leguminous, brightly colored flowers hang all over the branches before the green leaves unfurl.

This is a simple preparation that adds bright flavor and vitamin C to any savory meal. The flowers lend their color to the vinegar, giving a wonderful red-violet hue to this beloved pantry item. Sprinkle some of the capers on Nettle & Lovage Potato Soup (page 51) or Sizzling Garlic & Chili Noodles (page 58).

✿ **FORAGER'S NOTE** Collect enough of your unopened redbud flowers to fill a small jar with a lid. You will need to do your own research to ensure you are harvesting the correct flower, and please always make sure to harvest just what you need. This tree is generally prolific but is also a pollinator's paradise when other flowers are not open yet, so please remember to leave plenty on the tree.

» **SIMPLE SWAP** You can replace redbud flowers with dandelion buds or nasturtium buds, if available.

---

1 cup unopened redbud flowers

½ cup Champagne vinegar or white wine vinegar

½ cup filtered water

1 tablespoon sea salt

Place your flowers in a half-pint mason jar or other wide-mouth glass jar with a lid. Heat the vinegar and water in a small saucepan over medium heat. Stir in the salt, whisking until it dissolves. Let the brine cool completely and then pour it over the redbud flowers in the jar.

Cover the top of the jar with a square piece of parchment paper, then screw on the lid. The parchment will prevent the lid from corroding. Alternatively, you can use a noncorrosive lid. Place the jar in a cool and dark area or in the refrigerator for a day or two and shake daily. After a day or two, move the jar into the refrigerator. The capers are ready to eat right away and will last for several months in the refrigerator.

# PURPLE CURTIDO-CABBAGE QUICK PICKLE WITH OREGANO & CHILI

### MAKES 1 QUART-SIZE JAR

Curtido is a slightly spicy El Salvadorian quick pickle that adds incredible flavor to any meal and is traditionally served with pupusas, like those on page 94. It is a combination of cabbage, onion, carrots, and oregano. This is a fast and delicious recipe that can be made ahead of time and will keep great in the refrigerator for several weeks.

» **SIMPLE SWAPS** Substitute regular oregano for wild oregano, and green cabbage for purple.

½ large purple cabbage,
    sliced thinly

4 cups boiling water

½ medium to large yellow onion,
    sliced thinly

2 carrots, sliced into thin rounds

2 garlic cloves, chopped finely

2 tablespoons fresh wild oregano,
    or 1 tablespoon dried

1 jalapeño pepper, seeds removed
    and sliced thinly, or 1 teaspoon
    dried whole hot pepper

1 tablespoon salt

½ cup cider vinegar

Place the cabbage in a colander over the sink and pour the boiling water evenly over the top. This helps to soften and prepare it for the pickle. Run cold water over it for about a minute.

Stir together the cabbage and remaining ingredients in a large bowl. Then, transfer the mixture to a quart-size glass jar with a lid. Place the jar in the refrigerator or eat the pickle right away, but the flavors will intermingle and round out after a few days or a week.

# FLOWER & HERB HONEY

### MAKES ONE 8-OUNCE JAR

There is nothing quite as magic-filled or delectable as the flowers and herbs of summer preserved in honey—stirred into your favorite tea later in the year. Historically, honey was known as a food of the gods; it has been used for more than 8,000 years, both as a medicine and as a sweetener, deemed worthy of worship in some cultures. Honey has been used to treat moderate to severe infections, burns, and wounds, both internally and topically, and I always keep a jar on hand in my kitchen for burns. For this recipe, you can use whatever edible flower you prefer: rose petals, lilacs, violets, wild oregano, or dried herbs and flowers.

☀ FORAGER'S NOTE  If harvesting fresh flowers, gather them in the morning when they are most fragrant and full of water.

1 cup fresh rose petals, or 1 cup dried

1 cup honey, or enough to fill to the top of the jar

If you are using fresh flowers, lay out the petals on a clean, dry towel in a single layer overnight, to wilt. Place your flowers or herbs in a wide-mouth 8-ounce glass jar. Pour the honey over the plants and stir with a knife to get out all the air bubbles. Label, seal, and store for 4 to 8 weeks.

It is recommended that you strain the flowers after 8 weeks, but I often leave mine in the jar to eat for a taste of summer in the depths of winter.

# SALT-CURED GREEN CORIANDER "CAPERS"

## MAKES ONE 4- OR 8-OUNCE JAR

Coriander berries are my favorite salt cure, and I was drawn to them for their healing benefits, incredible scent, texture, and bright flavor. Inspired by the salt-curing traditions in Sicily, I created this recipe with the green seeds of the cilantro, or coriander, plant before they dried. Coriander is a medicinal powerhouse, rich in antioxidants and beneficial compounds that may lower blood sugar, reduce cholesterol, aid digestion, and support brain and heart health.

✷ **FORAGER'S NOTE** Harvest the seeds or berries of the coriander when they are green and fresh. Dried coriander berries will not work in this recipe.

» **SIMPLE SWAP** This recipe can also work with green elderberries (no stems or leaves), dandelion buds, or nasturtium buds.

---

3 to 7 tablespoons sea salt

¼ to ½ cup green coriander berries

Take a 4- or 8-ounce mason jar with a lid and layer a thin line, about 1 teaspoon, of the salt on the bottom. Add a layer of coriander berries, about 1 tablespoon, on top of the salt. Add 1 to 2 teaspoons of the salt, then another tablespoon of the berries, and continue to alternate layering salt and berries until the jar is filled, adding a thick layer of salt on the top. Cover with the lid and shake the jar a little. Take off the lid and add a little more salt to cover the berries. Cover the jar with a paper towel (not the lid) and secure it to the outer rim of the jar with a rubber band or the band of the lid. Place in an airy location that is not in direct sunlight.

Every day for about 5 days, drain away any water that comes from the berries by removing the paper towel and holding or pressing the top of the berries to squeeze it a bit. After it has stopped yielding liquid, cover with the lid and store in a cool, dark place for up to 6 months or longer. Rinse the berries when you are ready to use them, and blend them into marinades, dressings, or just add them into main dishes for a pop of flavor and depth.

# WILDFLOWER FINISHING SALTS

**MAKES APPROXIMATELY 1 CUP**

Flower and herb finishing salts are colorful ways to add flavor, phytochemicals, and beauty to meals, as well as preserving the harvest. Color is one of the most important ways we can convey a story of the plants, and salt is the perfect medium.

Salt was discovered when people began following larger animals to natural salt licks in the wild. Within a short time, salt became a currency, wars were fought over it, and it was traded for more than gold. Salt is an especially magical element in alchemy, associated with the ouroboros, the snake eating its own tail, and is known as one of the essential elements of transformation. But salt also activates our taste buds, bringing everything alive in our food; it preserves and cures foods, while unlocking incredible flavors. Use any edible herb or flower in this recipe, adjusting the amount of salt more or less depending on the moisture in your flowers or herbs. You want it to have the consistency of lightly wet sand.

1 cup fine-grind sea salt, plus more as needed

1 cup fresh calendula, rose, butterfly pea flower, marigold petals, or other edible flower of your choice

Place the salt and fresh petals in a food processor or spice grinder; even a clean coffee grinder will work in batches. Grind until combined completely, adding more salt until the mixture is like wet sand.

Spread the mixture on a baking sheet in a thin layer and let dry for about a week, stirring the salt around with a fork twice a day to keep it fresh and prevent clumping. Store in a pint- or quart-size glass jar once it's completely dry. Label and enjoy within 6 months.

# FLAVORFUL MUSHROOM POWDERS

**MAKES APPROXIMATELY 1 CUP**

Mushroom powders have been one of the most essential items in my pantry for the last 15 years. When I began harvesting porcini mushrooms, I quickly learned that although they are astonishingly delicious as a fresh mushroom, drying and powdering them carried them into every season. I use the powder in making pastas; it goes in slow cooker broths, soups, marinades, breads, and sauces. The complexity and umami flavor that mushrooms can add to meals when dried and powdered is unparalleled. It can be done with porcini, truffle, shiitake, lion's mane, or any other edible variety.

1 cup mushrooms of your choice, dried and broken up into smaller pieces

If mushrooms are not dried, they must be sliced thinly and dried in a dehydrator or very slowly on a baking sheet in an oven at the lowest possible setting. Mushrooms can also be dried slowly on screens with good airflow outside in the sunlight, which has been shown to increase their vitamin D content. Make sure that mushrooms are completely dry before grinding and storing, or they will mold.

Blend a handful of dried mushrooms in a blender, spice grinder, or coffee grinder until they are completely powdered. Store in a sealed and labeled jar.

# FORAGER'S EVERYTHING SALT BLEND

**MAKES APPROXIMATELY 1 CUP**

I created this blend to add some of my favorite foraged seeds, seaweeds, and plants to an already favorite seasoning, and it is the most-used condiment in our pantry now.

A main component of this blend is the pan-toasted black and white sesame seeds. Black sesame seeds are one of the oldest cultivated plants on earth, containing an incredible amount of essential vitamins and minerals, including substantial amounts of calcium. In Japan, sesame seeds, in the form of gomasio, are a popular addition to meals that inspired the seaweed addition in this blend. This is the main salt blend that is always on my kitchen table. It goes on toast, veggies, popcorn, anything savory.

1 tablespoon black sesame seeds

1 tablespoon white sesame seeds

1 tablespoon poppy seeds

1 tablespoon nettle seeds

1 tablespoon seaweed, blended into small bits: I use two kinds of foraged Irish seaweed called sweet dilisk and sea truffle

1 tablespoon dehydrated garlic bits

1 tablespoon dehydrated onion bits

1 tablespoon coarse or fine sea salt

Pan-toast the sesame seeds together, stirring constantly, in a small skillet over medium heat until they begin to release their scent, 2 to 5 minutes. Pour them onto a plate to cool them completely before mixing them with the other ingredients.

Combine all the ingredients in a medium bowl. Transfer to a jar and label. This blend will keep for at least 6 months. Add to everything: salads, soups, on veggies, potatoes, toast, noodles, bagels (such as the ones on page 144), and more.

# LACTO-FERMENTED GREEN TOMATO CHUTNEY

### MAKES 1 QUART-SIZE JAR

This is a piquant, delicious chutney made from unripe tomatoes inevitably hanging on the vine at the end of summer. In some places, such as the southern United States, these green tomatoes are sold in the grocery store toward the end of summer, and they can occasionally be found at farmers' markets or from friends or neighbors growing tomatoes. Green tomatoes are rich in vitamins A, C, and E, and are slightly sour and crisp. This recipe can be made as a lacto-ferment, meaning it contains probiotic benefits, or it can be made quickly to eat right away.

6 cups green tomatoes, chopped roughly

1½ to 2 cups fresh cilantro

2 to 3 tablespoons sea salt

3 to 5 garlic cloves, chopped roughly

1 small yellow onion, chopped roughly

1 to 2 hot peppers, chopped, or red pepper flakes

Combine all the ingredients in a blender and blend until well mixed but still textured. Transfer the mixture to a quart-size glass jar, filling to the top of the jar and sealing with a lid. If it doesn't fill to the top, then add a little water.

If you have a fermenting lid, use the fermenting lid for your jar. If you do not have a fermenting lid, just leave your jarred chutney on the counter for 48 hours and open it once or twice a day to let the pressure escape, sealing it right away afterward. After at least 48 hours, place your ferment in the refrigerator, where it will keep for 5 to 7 days. Use as a condiment on everything from soups to stews, or use as a dip.

**NOTES** Green tomatoes have been eaten all over the world in a variety of preparations, but there are compounds in green tomatoes that are known to be toxic at high levels, and can be irritating for some people.

For a nonfermented version of this recipe, reduce the salt quantity to 1 to 2 teaspoons, taste, add more salt as needed, and refrigerate immediately.

# LACTO-FERMENTED PURPLE DAIKON RADISH

### MAKES 1 QUART-SIZE JAR

Daikon radish is my favorite vegetable to eat as a lacto-ferment; its vibrant colors and lightly spicy flavor elevate any meal. A lacto-ferment is created simply with salt and the welcome proliferation of naturally occurring bacteria that's present on all plants. It is an alchemical process of making probiotic-rich vegetables for improved gut health. Fermented daikon radish is the perfect topping for toast, soups or stews, savory flatbreads or pancakes, noodle dishes, and more. Daikon radishes can be found in grocery stores, at farmers' markets, or grown in a garden beginning in the spring months and stretching into the late fall season.

» SIMPLE SWAP  Use any radish you have available in place of the purple daikon.

3 to 4 cups purple daikon radishes, peeled and shredded

2 to 3 cups spring water

2 tablespoons sea salt or kosher salt

Have ready a quart-size mason jar that has a fermentation lid. Place the shredded radishes in your jar, making sure they come up to the shoulder or curve of the jar. Add more shredded radish as needed.

Heat the spring or filtered water with the sea salt in a medium saucepan over medium heat until the salt is dissolved. Turn off the heat and wait for the salted water to cool. Once it is completely cooled, pour it over the radishes until they are fully submerged in the brine, and the liquid is nearly to the top of the jar.

Attach the fermentation lid as directed and ensure that all the radish is under the brine. Leave on your counter for 4 to 7 days, checking their flavor after 4 days. If the flavor is sour or tangy enough for you, replace the fermentation lid with the regular lid and place the jar in the refrigerator. If not, leave it on your counter to ferment for 2 to 3 more days. Fermentation will be faster or slower depending on the temperature of the room.

Once the radishes are fermented to your liking, remove the fermenting lid and place the jar in the refrigerator with a regular lid. Eat within 1 to 2 months for optimal crunch and flavor.

Lacto-Fermented Purple Daikon Radish

# PRESERVED MEYER LEMONS

### MAKES 1 QUART-SIZE JAR

Winter is citrus season, and it is the perfect time to make salt-preserved Meyer lemons to add to your pantry. I make preserved lemons in gallon measures in winter because they give an automatic depth and unique umami citrus flavor that elevates marinades, dressings, soups, and stews. They are lacto-fermented, using only salt as a preservative, resulting in beneficial probiotics that support the digestive system.

Preserved lemons have a long history of use, with written references as far back as 11th-century Arab-Mediterranean cuisine. Meyer lemons have a lightly floral scent and flavor, and have a thinner skin than regular lemons, but any lemon will work in this recipe, growing silky and soft in texture and mellowing in flavor over time.

One 32-ounce box kosher salt or sea salt

6 to 12 Meyer lemons, enough to fill a quart-size jar, plus more for juicing

Sprinkle a layer of salt, about 1 tablespoon, in the bottom of a quart-size mason jar.

Holding a lemon vertically on a cutting board, slice down to nearly separate into two halves, stopping about ½ inch before cutting all the way through the lemon. Rotate the lemon by 90 degrees and do the same again, cutting down until about ½ inch before the base. The lemon should be intact at the bottom and there are now four quarters, still attached at the base. Hold the lemon cut end up and pour 1 to 2 heaping teaspoons of salt into the sliced openings in the lemon, rubbing the salt into the crevices and giving it a light squeeze as you set it in the jar.

Continue in this way until the bottom layer of your jar is stuffed with salted lemons; two to three lemons will fit in the bottom. Pour at least 2 tablespoons of salt over this layer and continue to partially slice and salt the next layer of lemons, pouring a layer of salt over each layer of lemons, until the jar is filled. The lemons should be packed in tight so the juice is oozing out and beginning to cover them in brine.

If there is not enough liquid brine created at this point, juice a lemon or two and pour the fresh juice over the top of the lemons so the jar is full and the lemons are beneath the brine.

**VARIATIONS** Add spices and herbs, such as coriander seeds, bay leaves, red pepper flakes, black peppercorns, or fennel layered into the mixture of salt and lemons.

Seal and label your jar with the date, and leave it on the counter for about a week, making sure the lemons are always below the brine. Open the jar daily, to "burp" it, allowing any pressure to release that has built up. Seal it afterward and make sure the lemons are below the brine.

After 1 week, place the jar in the refrigerator and let the preserves mellow. I have kept and used my preserved lemons for well over a year. A favorite chef of mine has a jar that has been going for 5 years, unrefrigerated, with the most delicious preserved lemons I have tasted. I am not recommending this, but preserved lemons are a very acidic recipe that will be stable in the refrigerator for months, getting better over time.

To use, remove from your jar and rinse off excess salt if you desire. Dice or puree the lemons and add them to recipes.

# QUICK-PICKLED RED ONION WITH ROSE HIPS

### MAKES 1 PINT-SIZE JAR

Quick pickles are one of the best ways to preserve seasonal vegetables, while giving you colorful condiments that build flavor in any meal. Pickled red onion is a popular condiment, and it's a prebiotic food that contains high levels of quercetin, a beneficial compound that may be protective for the respiratory system and helpful for seasonal allergies. Rose hips are a perfect, lightly fruity addition to the traditional pickle. They add a boost of vitamin C to the red onions. These are a delicious and colorful addition to any savory meal.

» **SIMPLE SWAP** If you do not have seeded rose hips, use whole hips and just do not eat the seeds. They will still add flavor, vitamins, and minerals to your pickle. Do not use rose hips with spines or thorns on the outside, as those may be difficult to strain out.

½ cup cider vinegar

½ cup water

1 large red onion, sliced into rounds

½ teaspoon salt

1 teaspoon honey

1 garlic clove, smashed

2 tablespoons rose hips, seeded

Heat the vinegar and water in a saucepan over medium heat until simmering. Add the red onion and cook for about 10 seconds, then turn off the heat. Stir in the salt and honey until dissolved.

Layer the garlic and rose hips into a pint-size mason jar and scoop the onions and hot liquid over the top. Label with the date and contents, seal with a lid, and place in the refrigerator. The pickle will be ready to add to dishes after 2 hours, but can be kept, refrigerated, for up to 4 weeks. The onions will mellow over the course of a couple of days.

**VARIATIONS** Once the garlic and rose hips have been placed in the jar, add 1 tablespoon of lemonade sumac or staghorn sumac berries, 1 teaspoon of lemon or other citrus zest, 1 teaspoon of dried wild or regular oregano, a pinch of hot red chili powder, 1 teaspoon of yellow or brown mustard seeds, and/or ½ teaspoon of black peppercorns.

# ROSE HIP & GINGER OXYMEL

**MAKES ABOUT 1½ PINTS**

One of my favorite medicines to work with in any season is the oxymel, an ancient herbal remedy composed of plants, vinegar, and honey. Aside from the beauty and flavor they impart, rose hips contain high amounts of vitamin C and are one of the only plants we can forage into the winter months. They also contain a surprising amount of B vitamins, polyphenols, and vitamins A and E, all of which have immunity-boosting and antioxidant properties. Raw cider vinegar may be supportive for gut health, and honey provides many antiviral and antibacterial benefits.

Rose hip oxymel has a slightly fruity and tart flavor, warmed by the ginger and cinnamon, perfect for a sparkling drink, dressings, or warm drinks.

» **SIMPLE SWAPS** If you prefer a less sweet version, just use the vinegar without the honey, or add a smaller amount of sweetener to the vinegar. Use dried rose hips in place of the fresh hips.

1 cup fresh rose hips

1 to 2 slices fresh ginger, about a tablespoon

1 cinnamon stick

1 to 2 cups raw cider vinegar

½ to 1 cup honey

Place the rose hips, ginger, and cinnamon stick in a pint-size glass jar, filling the jar about two-thirds of the way. Cover in cider vinegar to the top of the jar. Add a square of wax or parchment paper to the top before you screw on the lid, to prevent corrosion of the metal lid. Label and place in a cool, dark space for 4 to 8 weeks.

Strain the oxymel through a fine-mesh sieve, cheesecloth, coffee filter, or clean muslin towel, reserving the liquid. This is a very important step, as rose hip seeds have irritating hairs that we want to filter out. You can strain a second time to be sure you've removed more of the hairs.

Now, mix about half as much honey as you have of the vinegar into the strained vinegar (for instance, if you have 2 cups of vinegar, add 1 cup of honey). Use more or less honey depending on your tastes and desired sweetness. Label and seal the jar again, storing it in a cool and dark space. Vinegar extractions do not require refrigeration. The oxymel is now ready to use.

Take a teaspoon daily in water, stir into teas or sparkling drinks, and use in salad dressings, marinades, or as a replacement for vinegar in a recipe.

# ACKNOWLEDGMENTS

"I live my life in widening circles
that reach out across the world."
—RAINER MARIA RILKE

THIS BOOK IS A LIFELONG DREAM COME TRUE, and I am infinitely grateful to the Land, the Water, the Plants, my teachers, my ancestors, and the loved ones who have supported and shared in this journey along the way. I am eternally grateful to my daughter, Nila Marina, and the wisdom, brilliance, beauty, perspective, and generous heart she has shared with me since the moment she arrived; I love you infinitely my Pi girl. To my husband, Mark DeRespinis, for dancing this spiral, flowering road with me, holding seeds in our mouths and dreams in our hearts and for growing the most beautiful and loved plants year after year at Esoterra Culinary Gardens. Thank you to my mom, Debbie Lanich, for teaching me to taste every food, being my greatest fan and my first baking teacher. Thank you to my dad, Rich LaBrie, for being the best father in the world, for loving every burnt cookie I ever made, for reminding me why I am here, and bringing me to the water and the West, where I made my home. To my grandma, Jeanette LaBrie, for the summers, the magic, story, awe, hatching butterflies, catching frogs, and everything I love most about food; I miss you always and feel you with me. Grateful always to the land I have lived on in Española, New Mexico, to the Tewa Pueblo, and to the Ute, Arapahoe, and Cheyenne Nation Land of Colorado. So many people have guided and supported this path and I am forever grateful: To my grandparents: Anne and Oscar Lanich and Jeanette and Roland "Jack" LaBrie. To my godmother and godfather, Nancy and Howard Waxman, and Uncle Hector Caldera. To my dearest friends and teachers: David Arfa, Rachel Weitz, Dan Halpern, Emunah, Alicia Banister, Holly Takoda Rhoads, Adrienne Sloan, Hope, Leland, Kaleia, Jade Bird, and Crystal Guthrie-Logghe, Koko, Ariana Rossi, Megan Dyer, Ann Drucker, Greg Schoen, Carl White Eagle Barnes, Gerry Snyder, Betsy Bergstrom, Heather Powell,

Elizabeth Wilson-Levy, Annie Lederman, Ayala Heller, Corina Logghe, Joan and Mike Logghe, Carol Nieukirk, Thea Schnase, Gail Margolis, Nick Polizzi, Michelle Polizzi for so much of the beautiful pottery in this book, Lee Greenberg, Paige Turner, Charlie Philbrick, Zephir Plume and Stephanie Sutten, and all The Wednesday and Thursday Diners, and to my Chicago Beach Family-I love you all: Clark and Sandy DuBois, Alan and Barbara Golden, Ken Sohn and Annalynn Christoff, Dawn Booras, Barb and Mike Murray, Ellen Iverson, Robb Cole. Thank you to everyone that has supported this work through social media, Patreon, and my classes; I am so grateful. Go raibh míle maith agaibh to Hili and Feargus MacDaeid, Lucy O'Hagan, Rob Dunne, Cathy Dunne, and the plants, story, language, and land of Ériu/Ireland. Thank you to my agent, Joy Tutela; my editor, Isabel McCarthy; and everyone at Norton and Countryman Press for supporting this book.

# INDEX

Page numbers in **bold** indicate illustrations and page numbers in *italics* indicate tables.